MW01078666

The Official Rails-to-Trails Conservancy Guidebook

Rail-Trails
Iowa &
Missouri

The definitive guide to the region's top multiuse trails

 WILDERNESS PRESS ... *on the trail since 1967*

Rail-Trails: Iowa & Missouri

Copyright © 2017 by Rails-to-Trails Conservancy

Maps: Lohnes+Wright; map data courtesy of Environmental Systems Research Institute
Cover design: Scott McGrew
Book design: Annie Long; book layout: Leslie Shaw

Cataloging-in-Publication Data is available from the Library of Congress

ISBN 9780899978468 (pbk.); ISBN 9780899978475 (ebook); 9780899979342 (hardcover)

Published by: ♠ **WILDERNESS PRESS**
An imprint of AdventureKEEN
2204 First Ave. S, Ste. 102
Birmingham, AL 35233
800-443-7227; fax 205-326-1012

Visit **wildernesspress.com** for a complete listing of our books and for ordering information. Contact us at our website, at **facebook.com/wildernesspress1967**, or at **twitter
.com/wilderness1967** with questions or comments. To find out more about who we are
and what we're doing, visit **blog.wildernesspress.com.**

Distributed by Publishers Group West

Front cover photo: MKT Nature and Fitness Trail, page 137, photographed by Michael
Friedman; *Back cover photo*: High Trestle Trail, page 42, photographed by Milo Bateman

SAFETY NOTICE: Although Wilderness Press and Rails-to-Trails Conservancy have
made every attempt to ensure that the information in this book is accurate at press time,
they are not responsible for any loss, damage, injury, or inconvenience that may occur to
anyone while using this book. You are responsible for your own safety and health while in
the wilderness. The fact that a trail is described in this book does not mean that it will be
safe for you. Be aware that trail conditions can change from day to day. Always check local
conditions, know your own limitations, and consult a map.

About Rails-to-Trails Conservancy

Headquartered in Washington, D.C., Rails-to-Trails Conservancy (RTC) is a nonprofit organization dedicated to creating a nationwide network of trails from former rail lines and connecting corridors to build healthier places for healthier people.

Railways helped build America. Spanning from coast to coast, these ribbons of steel linked people, communities, and enterprises, spurring commerce and forging a single nation that bridges a continent. But in recent decades, many of these routes have fallen into disuse, severing communal ties that helped bind Americans together.

When RTC opened its doors in 1986, the rail-trail movement was in its infancy. Most projects focused on single, linear routes in rural areas, created for recreation and conservation. RTC sought broader protection for the unused corridors, incorporating rural, suburban, and urban routes.

Year after year, RTC's efforts to protect and align public funding with trail building created an environment that allowed trail advocates in communities across the country to initiate trail projects. These ever-growing ranks of trail professionals, volunteers, and RTC supporters have built momentum for the national rail-trails movement. As the number of supporters multiplied, so too did rail-trails.

Americans now enjoy more than 22,000 miles of open rail-trails, and as they flock to the trails to connect with family members and friends, enjoy nature, and get to places in their local neighborhoods and beyond, their economic prosperity, health, and overall well-being continue to flourish.

A signature endeavor of RTC is **TrailLink.com**, America's portal to these rail-trails as well as other multiuse trails. When RTC launched **TrailLink.com** in 2000, our organization was one of the first to compile such detailed trail information on a national scale. Today, the website continues to play a critical role in both encouraging and satisfying the country's growing need for opportunities to ride, walk, skate, or run for recreation or transportation. This free trail-finder database—which includes detailed descriptions, interactive maps, photo galleries, and first-hand ratings and reviews—can be used as a companion resource to the trails in this guidebook.

The national voice for more than 160,000 members and supporters, RTC is committed to ensuring a better future for America made possible by trails and the connections they inspire. Learn more at **railstotrails.org**.

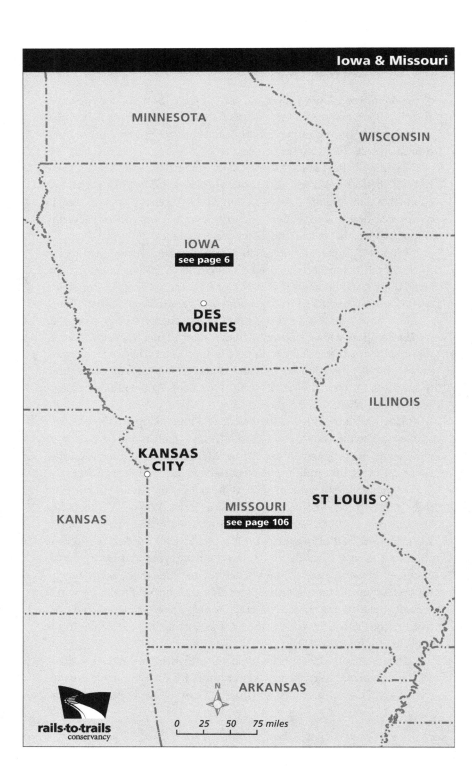

MINNESOTA

WISCONSIN

IOWA
see page 6

○
DES
MOINES

ILLINOIS

KANSAS
CITY
○

ST LOUIS ○

KANSAS

MISSOURI
see page 106

N

ARKANSAS

0   25   50   75 miles

rails·to·trails
conservancy

Table of Contents

IOWA 6

MISSOURI 106

Foreword

For those of you who have already experienced the sheer enjoyment and freedom of riding on a rail-trail, welcome back! You'll find this *Rail-Trails Iowa & Missouri* guidebook to be a useful and fun guide to your favorite trails, as well as an introduction to pathways you have yet to travel.

For readers who are discovering for the first time the adventures possible on a rail-trail, thank you for joining the rail-trail movement. Since 1986, Rails-to-Trails Conservancy has been the leading supporter and defender of these priceless public corridors. We are excited to bring you *Rail-Trails Iowa & Missouri* so you, too, can enjoy some of the region's premier rail-trails and multiuse trails. These hiking and biking trails are ideal ways to connect with your community, with nature, and with your friends and family.

I've found that trails have a way of bringing people together, and as you'll see from this book, you have opportunities in every state you visit to get on a great trail. Whether you're looking for a place to exercise, explore, commute, or play, there is a trail in this book for you.

So I invite you to sit back, relax, pick a trail that piques your interest—and then get out, get active, and have some fun. I'll be out on the trails too, so be sure to wave as you go by.

Happy trails,

Keith Laughlin, President
Rails-to-Trails Conservancy

Acknowledgments

Many thanks to the following contributors and to all the trail managers we called on for assistance to ensure the maps, photographs, and trail descriptions are as accurate as possible:

Ashley Ashworth

Milo Bateman

Elton Clark

Tracy Conoboy

Ryan Cree

Cindy Dickerson

Eli Griffen

Katie Guerin

Brandi Horton

Brian Housh

Amy Kapp

Joe LaCroix

Jake Laughlin

Suzanne Matyas

Cam McKinney

Molly McKinney

Eric Oberg

Liz Sewell

Leeann Sinpatanasakul

Laura Stark

Derek Strout

Danielle Taylor

Ana Valenzuela

Introduction

In *Rail-Trails Iowa & Missouri,* we highlight 44 of the region's top rail-trails and other multiuse pathways, including Katy Trail State Park, which spans nearly the entire state of Missouri and is the country's longest contiguous rail-trail. The Katy Trail has an honored place in the Rail-Trail Hall of Fame, as does another trail in this book, Iowa's Wabash Trace Nature Trail.

Both Iowa and Missouri have a rich railroad history, which is remembered and celebrated with nearly 1,300 miles of rail-trail between the two states. In 1856, the first trains to ever cross the mighty Mississippi River entered Davenport, Iowa, ushering in a new wave of east-west travel and commerce across the burgeoning nation. In Missouri, the important role of St. Louis as a steamboat port by the 1840s made it an opportune hub for the railroads that came later and radiated outward from the city.

In the United States, there are now more than 2,000 rail-trails utilizing former rail corridors, such as Missouri's new Rock Island Spur, which officially opened in December 2016 and stretches nearly 50 miles from a connection with the Katy Trail in Windsor to the outskirts of the Kansas City metro area.

Iowa's longest completed rail-trail, the Raccoon River Valley Trail, boasts nearly 90 miles of paved pathway through some of the state's most picturesque landscapes: woodlands, prairie, bucolic fields, and small Midwestern towns. For an unusual and memorable sight, don't miss the High Trestle Trail and its jaw-dropping bridge towering 130 feet above the Des Moines River.

Those who would prefer a waterfront experience can explore the Mississippi River Trail, which runs from Riverdale to Davenport along the river and provides a platform to enjoy parks, festivals, and music and sporting events. In Missouri, the St. Louis Riverfront Trail swings by the famed Gateway Arch and follows the Mississippi, while the Riverfront Heritage Trail is nestled in the heart of Kansas City on the opposite end of the state.

No matter which routes in *Rail-Trails Iowa & Missouri* you choose, you'll experience the unique history, culture, and geography of each, as well as the communities that have built and embraced them.

What Is a Rail-Trail?

Rail-trails are multiuse public paths built along former railroad corridors. Most often flat or following a gentle grade, they are suited to walking, running, cycling, mountain biking, in-line skating, cross-country skiing, horseback riding, and wheelchair use. Since the 1960s, Americans have created more than 22,000 miles of rail-trails throughout the country.

These extremely popular recreation and transportation corridors traverse urban, suburban, and rural landscapes. Many preserve historical landmarks, while others serve as wildlife conservation corridors, linking isolated parks and establishing greenways in developed areas. Rail-trails also stimulate local economies by boosting tourism and promoting trailside businesses.

What Is a Rail-with-Trail?

A rail-with-trail is a public path that parallels a still-active rail line. Some run adjacent to high-speed, scheduled trains, often linking public transportation stations, while others follow tourist routes and slow-moving excursion trains. Many share an easement, separated from the rails by extensive fencing. More than 275 rails-with-trails exist in the United States.

*R*ail-Trails Iowa & Missouri provides the information you'll need to plan a rewarding trek on a rail-trail or other multiuse trail in the region. With words to inspire you and maps to chart your path, it makes choosing the best route a breeze. Following are some of the highlights.

Maps

You'll find three levels of maps in this book: an **overall regional map, state locator maps,** and **detailed trail maps.**

The trails in this guide are located in Iowa and Missouri. Each chapter details a particular state's network of trails, marked on locator maps in the chapter introduction. Use these maps to find the trails nearest you, or select several neighboring trails and plan a weekend hiking or biking excursion. Once you find a trail on a state locator map, simply flip to the corresponding page number for a full description. Accompanying trail maps mark each route's access roads, trailheads, parking areas, restrooms, and other defining features.

Key to Map Icons

| Parking | Drinking Water | Restrooms | Featured Trail | Connecting Trail | Active Railroad |

Trail Descriptions

*T*rails are listed in alphabetical order within each chapter. Each description leads off with a set of summary information, including trail endpoints and mileage, a roughness index, the trail surface, and possible uses.

The map and summary information list the trail endpoints (either a city, street, or more specific location), with suggested points from which to start and finish. Additional access points are marked on the maps and mentioned in the trail descriptions. The maps and descriptions also highlight available amenities, including parking and restrooms, as well as such area attractions as shops, services, museums, parks, and stadiums. Trail length is listed in miles.

Each trail has a **roughness index** rating from 1 to 3. A rating of 1 indicates a smooth, level surface that is accessible to users of all ages and abilities. A 2 rating means the surface may be loose and/or uneven and could pose a problem for road bikes and wheelchairs. A 3 rating suggests a rough surface that is only recommended for mountain bikers and hikers. Surfaces can range from asphalt or concrete to ballast, boardwalk, cinder, crushed stone, gravel, grass, dirt, sand, and/or woodchips. Where relevant, trail descriptions address alternating surface conditions.

All trails are open to pedestrians, and most allow bicycles, except where noted in the trail summary or description. The summary also indicates wheelchair access. Other possible uses include in-line skating, fishing, horseback riding, mountain biking, cross-country skiing, and snowshoeing. While most trails are off-limits to motor vehicles, some local trail organizations do allow ATVs and snowmobiles.

Trail descriptions themselves suggest an ideal itinerary for each route, including the best parking areas and access points, where to begin, your direction of travel, and any highlights along the way. Following each description are directions to the recommended trailheads.

Each trail description also lists a local website for further information. Be sure to visit these websites in advance for updates and current conditions. **TrailLink.com** is another great resource for updated content on the trails in this guidebook.

Trail Use

Rail-trails are popular destinations for a range of users, often making them busy places to enjoy the outdoors. Following basic trail etiquette and safety guidelines will make your experience more pleasant.

- ➤ **Keep to the right,** except when passing.

- ➤ **Pass on the left,** and give a clear audible warning: "Passing on your left."

- ➤ **Be aware** of other trail users, particularly around corners and blind spots, and be especially careful when entering a trail, changing direction, or passing so that you don't collide with traffic.

- ➤ **Respect wildlife** and public and private property; leave no trace and take out litter.

- ➤ **Control your speed,** especially near pedestrians, playgrounds, and heavily congested areas.

- ➤ **Travel single file.** Cyclists and pedestrians should ride or walk single file in congested areas or areas with reduced visibility.

- ➤ **Cross carefully** at intersections; always look both ways and yield to through traffic. Pedestrians have the right-of-way.

- ➤ **Keep one ear open and volume low** on portable listening devices to increase your awareness of your surroundings.

- ➤ **Wear a helmet** and other safety gear if you're cycling or in-line skating.

➤ **Consider visibility.** Wear reflective clothing, use bicycle lights, or bring flashlights or helmet-mounted lights for tunnel passages or twilight excursions.

➤ **Keep moving,** and don't block the trail. When taking a rest, turn off the trail to the right. Groups should avoid congregating on or blocking the trails. If you have an accident on the trail, move to the right as soon as possible.

➤ **Bicyclists yield** to all other trail users. Pedestrians yield to horses. If in doubt, yield to all other trail users.

➤ **Dogs are permitted** on most trails, but some trails through parks, wildlife refuges, or other sensitive areas may not allow pets; it's best to check the trail website before your visit. If pets are permitted, keep your dog on a short leash and under your control at all times. Remove dog waste in a designated trash receptacle.

➤ **Teach your children** these trail essentials, and be especially diligent to keep them out of faster-moving trail traffic.

➤ **Be prepared,** especially on long-distance rural trails. Bring water, snacks, maps, a light source, matches, and other equipment you may need. Because some areas may not have good reception for cell phones, know where you're going, and tell someone else your plan.

Key to Trail Use

cycling   in-line skating   fishing   wheelchair access   horseback riding   mountain biking

snowmobiling   walking   cross-country skiing   ATV

Learn More

To learn about additional multiuse trails in your area or to plan a trip to an area beyond the scope of this book, visit Rails-to-Trails Conservancy's trailfinder website, **TrailLink.com,** a free resource with information on more than 30,000 miles of trails nationwide.

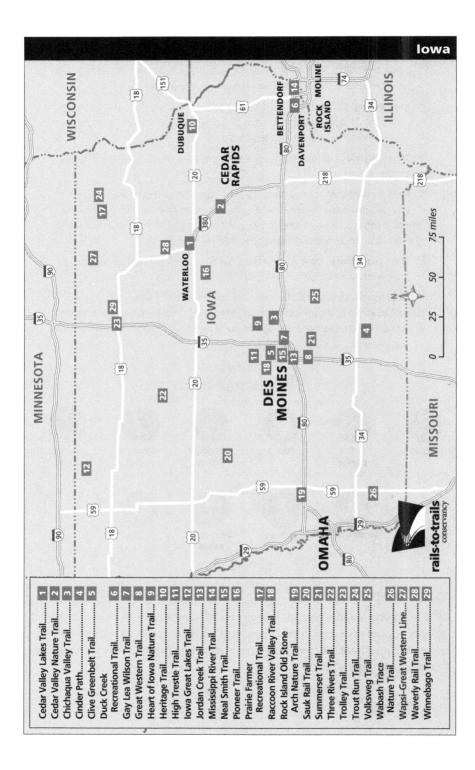

Iowa

Cedar Valley Lakes Trail	1
Cedar Valley Nature Trail	2
Chichaqua Valley Trail	3
Cinder Path	4
Clive Greenbelt Trail	5
Duck Creek Recreational Trail	6
Gay Lea Wilson Trail	7
Great Western Trail	8
Heart of Iowa Nature Trail	9
Heritage Trail	10
High Trestle Trail	11
Iowa Great Lakes Trail	12
Jordan Creek Trail	13
Mississippi River Trail	14
Neal Smith Trail	15
Pioneer Trail	16
Prairie Farmer Recreational Trail	17
Raccoon River Valley Trail	18
Rock Island Old Stone Arch Nature Trail	19
Sauk Rail Trail	20
Summerset Trail	21
Three Rivers Trail	22
Trolley Trail	23
Trout Run Trail	24
Volksweg Trail	25
Wabash Trace Nature Trail	26
Wapsi–Great Western Line	27
Waverly Rail Trail	28
Winnebago Trail	29

Iowa

A former railroad bridge is just one of many highlights of the nearly 63-mile Wabash Trace Nature Trail (see page 91).

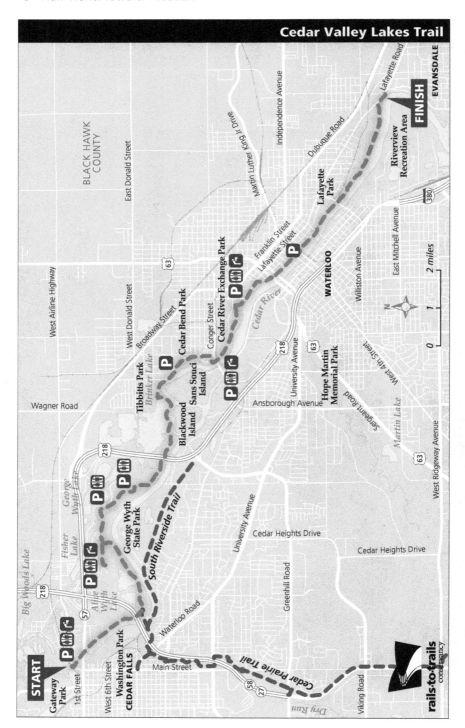

The name "Cedar Valley Lakes Trail" conjures images of lazy summer days by the river and magnificent fall leaf-peeping excursions. The actual experience doesn't disappoint; in fact, it exceeds expectations.

The trail—part of a 110-mile network of multiuse, soft, and emerging water trails—follows a heavily wooded route along the Cedar River, passing Alice Wyth Lake, Fisher Lake, George Wyth Lake, and Brinker Lake. The opportunities for recreation are limitless, with fishing, camping, picnicking, swimming, and more to entice outdoor enthusiasts.

Depart from Cedar Falls at Gateway Park, which has a playground, ice skating (in winter months), restrooms, and parking. The trail begins in a wooded area that offers connections to hiking trails and plenty of benches for rest and respite. Stay aware as you approach US 218; the trail—which continues on the opposite side of the road—is not well marked. Stay right to follow the trail under the overpass. Just 3 miles into the trip, a noteworthy diversion is

Lakes encapsulate a large portion of the 11.3-mile trail.

County
Black Hawk

Endpoints
Gateway Park at Lincoln St. and E. Main St. (Cedar Falls) to Randall Ave. and Lafayette Road (Evansdale)

Mileage
11.3

Type
Greenway/Non-Rail-Trail

Roughness Index
1

Surface
Asphalt, Concrete

Alice Wyth Lake, where there is a fishing jetty and an accessible shoreline. Alice Wyth Lake is immediately followed by George Wyth State Park and Lake, which features a popular beach for locals; here, you can picnic, camp, play on the jungle gym, fish, or swim. This state park also offers a unique perk: It connects to the Cedar Valley Paddlers Trail, a water trail that starts at Fisher Lake in the state park.

The trail takes you past Tibbitts Park and into downtown Cedar Falls and Waterloo, after which it passes Riverfront Stadium and runs through a small, quiet neighborhood for a short distance. You'll pick up the trail again at Cedar River Exchange Park, which offers riverfront amenities, including picnic areas, sports fields, a skate park, boating areas, and more.

Continue past the park to downtown Waterloo, where you'll find plenty of places to eat, grab a cup of coffee, or purchase a tasty treat. You may want to partake in many of the outdoor festivals hosted in downtown Waterloo during spring, summer, and fall, or just take in the history of the town by checking out one of several historical markers, such as the Vietnam Memorial dedicated to those Iowans who served in the war, or the marker remembering the great floods of 1858, 1929, and 1961. Part of the trail is built on top of the town's levee, which is tastefully landscaped with a variety of vegetation, flowers, and lighting. After Waterloo, the trail continues 3.2 miles to its endpoint in Evansdale.

Note: Fishing licenses are $9.50 per day and are available from the Iowa Department of Natural Resources. For more information, go to iowadnr.gov/Fishing/Fishing-Licenses-Laws/Additional-Regulations/Fishing-Licenses. In some parks, swimming is strictly prohibited. Follow posted rules for each park facility.

CONTACT: **cedartrailspartnership.org**

DIRECTIONS

To reach the western trailhead at Gateway Park in Cedar Falls from IA 58, take the exit for IA 57 toward Cedar Falls. Go 1.3 miles, and turn right onto Main St. Go 0.2 mile, and turn right onto Lincoln St. Turn right into the trailhead parking lot.

The closest parking at the southeast part of the trail is in Waterloo. To reach the parking lot from I-380, follow the route to US 218, and continue on US 218 N for 1.3 miles. Keep right to continue on Washington St. for 0.2 mile. Turn right onto W. Sixth St. Go 0.4 mile, and turn right into the trail parking lot at the intersection with Water St. If you pass the University of Northern Iowa Center for Urban Education, you have gone too far. The endpoint is located 2.5 miles southeast along the trail at Randall Ave.

The Cedar Valley Nature Trail—part of the cross-country American Discovery Trail—follows the fertile Cedar River between Evansdale and Ely. The nearly 68-mile trail comprises three former trails—the Cedar Valley Nature Trail, Cedar River Trail, and parts of the Hoover Nature Trail—which merged in spring 2017. The trail also includes an additional segment constructed in summer 2017 between Rowley Street in Ely and Linn County's southern border at Seven Sisters Road.

Among the first rail-trail conversions in the state, the northern portion traces the original corridor of the Waterloo, Cedar Falls and Northern Railway, an interurban railroad that, by 1914, had connected Cedar Rapids and Waterloo. The Illinois Central Railroad gained sole ownership in 1968 and abandoned large sections in 1983. The southern portion follows the old Burlington, Cedar Rapids and Northern Railway that operated from 1876 until 1903,

True to its name, the Cedar Valley Nature Trail follows the fertile land along the Cedar River.

Counties
Benton, Black Hawk, Buchanan, Linn

Endpoints
River Road and I-380 (Evansdale) to Seven Sisters Road and Ely Road (Ely)

Mileage
67.8

Type
Rail-Trail, On-Road Detour

Roughness Index
1–2

Surface
Asphalt, Crushed Stone

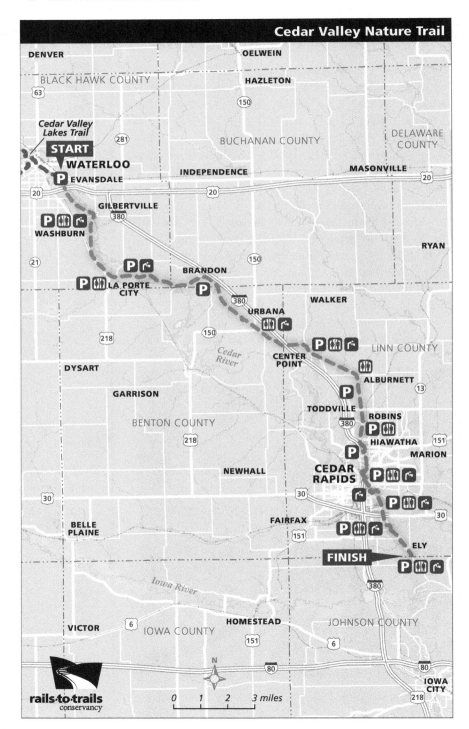

when it was acquired by the Chicago, Rock Island and Pacific Railroad. That railroad's bankruptcy in the early 1980s led to the line's abandonment, and a citizens' coalition launched efforts to acquire the railbed for a recreational trail.

Asphalt covers the northern 16-mile section of trail, as well as the southern section spanning from Iowa Street in Center Point to the Linn County Line. Occasional flooding can cause washouts along the trail or damage bridges (note that a 9-mile detour avoids a damaged bridge in La Porte). Parts of the trail are landscaped with grasses and wildflowers native to the Iowa prairie, providing habitat for the various songbirds and mammals that live along the corridor; it is not uncommon to see Iowa's state bird, the American Goldfinch. Cross-country skiing is permitted—except for on the portion of trail in Linn County.

At the northern trailhead on River Road (south of I-380), a paved connector trail joins the Cedar Valley Lakes Trail (see page 8) that leads to a trail system in Waterloo and Cedar Falls. Beginning at the northern trailhead, you'll head southeast over the Cedar River and along a 4.5-mile stretch to Gilbertville, where a trailhead at East Washburn Road offers restrooms, water, and parking.

From here, it's another 8 miles south to La Porte City. *Note:* the circa 1914 Wolf Creek Bridge in La Porte was closed after an engineering study reported structural problems in 2015, and the county has created a 9-mile detour on county roads until a more permanent fix can be found. In La Porte, you'll find food and refreshments, as well as a park offering shade at Maple and Walnut Streets (next to a rail yard). An old Chicago, Rock Island & Pacific Railroad depot is located in the rail yard, and a Waterloo, Cedar Falls and Northern Railway station dating from 1912 is located at the corner of Main and Locust Streets.

From La Porte, you'll head about 3 miles to a new bridge over a second Cedar River crossing (look for the red cedar trees that give the river its name). You'll then head east along oxbow lakes and through woodlands to two rural towns, Brandon and Urbana, both of which have markets. This northern section of trail is an important habitat for nesting waterfowl and songbirds.

In Center Point, you'll find a museum in the old railroad depot that's open on summer Sundays. Food and beverages are also available in town. You'll then head south along a rural stretch—look for deer, wild turkeys, and other wild animals—before reaching suburban Hiawatha. The trail runs below power lines as it heads into town; note that the Boyson Road trailhead offers a bike repair station, as well as water, restrooms, and parking.

Continue south past Cedar Lake to a seven-block stretch in downtown Cedar Rapids, host to a variety of restaurants, cultural attractions, and bars. At Seventh Street, the trail turns right, heads three blocks to the Cedar River, and then cuts left to follow the river a short distance. At 16th Avenue SW, the trail turns right, crosses over the Cedar River, and then follows it southeast until Tait Cummins Memorial Park, where it passes through a couple of tree-lined segments.

Making your way toward Ely, at the southern end of the Cedar Rapids metropolitan area, you'll enter a section where you can see for miles; look for a wind turbine or two on the distant horizon. Where the trail crosses Ely Road and Wright Brothers Boulevard, a plaque explains the area's unique landscape formed by two distinct landforms: open plains and pahas, which are hills formed by windblown silt. You'll then pass through Iowa farmland and subdivisions, eventually reaching City Park at Hillcrest Street. Here, you'll find a pond, restrooms, water, and parking.

The original section of trail turned right onto Dow Street, then left onto Main Street, and ended about 200 feet south of Rowley Street in Ely. In summer 2017, an additional segment was constructed extending the trail along Ely Road to the Linn County southern border at Seven Sisters Road.

CONTACT: mycountyparks.com/County/Linn/Park/Cedar-Valley-Nature-Trail.aspx or mycountyparks.com/County/Black-Hawk/Park/Cedar-Valley-Nature -Trail-Evansdale.aspx or linncountytrails.org/maps/find-a-trail /hoover-trail

DIRECTIONS

To reach the northern trailhead in Evansdale from I-380, take Exit 70, and head north on River Forest Road. Go 0.2 mile, and turn right onto Gilbert Drive; then go 0.9 mile, and turn right onto Grand Blvd. Go 0.2 mile, and bear left onto Sixth St. Bear right onto River Road, go 0.4 mile, and look for the trailhead parking on the left.

To reach the Boyson Road trailhead in Hiawatha from I-380, take Exit 25 onto Boyson Road, and head east. Go 0.3 mile, and turn right onto Kainz Drive; then turn left immediately into the trailhead parking lot. The trail passes in back of the lot.

To reach the southern trailhead in Ely from I-380 S/IA 27 S, take Exit 13 toward The Eastern Iowa Airport, and take a sharp left onto Wright Brothers Blvd. W. Go 3.8 miles, and turn right onto Ely Road. After 2.5 miles (Ely Road becomes State St. for 1.5 miles and then becomes Ely Road again), turn left onto Seven Sisters Road. Look for the trailhead on the left.

The paved Chichaqua Valley Trail crosses 27 miles of central Iowa farmland between the northeastern Des Moines suburbs and the rural community of Baxter. The trail's name, pronounced chee-chak-wah, is derived from a Native American word. Pioneers mistook it to mean skunk, but actually it refers to the aroma of wild onions that grew along the Skunk River, which the trail spans.

The trail follows the original route of the Wisconsin, Iowa & Nebraska Railroad, built in 1885. Other railroads to subsequently use the corridor include the Chicago, St. Paul, & Kansas City Railroad (1886–1892), the Chicago Great Western Company (1892–1968), and the Chicago & Northwestern Railroad Company (1968–1984). Abandoned in 1984, the route became one of Iowa's first rail-trail conversions in 1987. A 6-mile extension ushered the trail into Des Moines in 2015.

Counties
Jasper, Polk

Endpoints
NE 29th St. between NE 54th Ave. and NE 49th Ave. (Des Moines) to W. State St. between Railroad St. and N. Main St. (Baxter)

Mileage
27

Type
Rail-Trail

Roughness Index
2

Surface
Asphalt

East of Bondurant, the Chichaqua Valley Trail leaves urban landscapes behind.

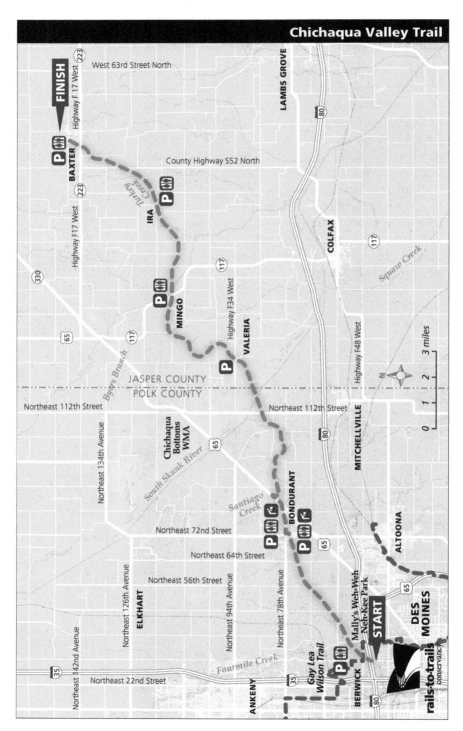

Although the trail is paved, the inconsistent surfaces at the eastern end of the trail make for rough traveling between Baxter and Mingo. The trail surface is much smoother and trailside services are more frequent west of Mingo. The trail crosses gravel roads every few miles, but the crossings are easy, and for most of the trail there is no noise but the wind rushing past. You can gauge your progress by watching for old railroad mile markers that show the distance to Kansas City.

Beginning at Mally's Weh-Weh-Neh-Kee Park (meaning "good place") in the former coal-mining community of Berwick, the junction with the Gay Lea Wilson Trail (see page 27) is 0.8 mile to the west and the trail end is 0.3 mile beyond that. Heading east, you'll leave behind suburban sprawl and pass farms before arriving at Bondurant in about 5 miles. The town completed the trailhead park, featuring a replica train depot for restrooms and drinking water, in 2013.

You might spot wildlife and wildflowers as the curvy route passes through the Santiago Creek greenbelt east of town. In about 7 miles you'll cross the Skunk River railroad bridge that dates to 1885 and enter the Chichaqua Wildlife Management Area.

The trail takes a serpentine course through the creek drainages and river valleys that is uncharacteristic of the straight routes charted by many Midwestern rail-trails. The next three small towns—Valeria, Mingo, and Ira—don't offer much in the way of food or refreshments over the next 15 miles.

Arriving at the end of the trail in Baxter, you'll be greeted by a restored 1913 wooden caboose that also contains historical displays and restrooms. Baxter offers cafés, taverns, and markets to replenish weary travelers.

CONTACT: www.polkcountyiowa.gov/conservation/parks-trails/5-chichaqua
-valley-trail

DIRECTIONS

To reach the southwestern trailhead at Mally's Weh-Weh-Neh-Kee Park from I-35, take Exit 89, and go east on Corporate Woods Drive toward the driver's license center. Go 0.8 mile, and continue on the road as it becomes SE 72nd St./NE 62nd Ave. Go 0.9 mile, and turn right onto NE Berwick Drive/County Road F52. Go 0.5 mile, and turn right into Mally's Park. Go about 200 feet, and find parking on the left. Follow the path heading northwest to the trail from the parking lot. The endpoint is located 1.2 miles southwest at NE 29th St.

To reach the northeastern trailhead from I-80, take Exit 149, and go north on NE 112th St./County Road S27. Go 5.8 miles, and turn right onto US 65/IA 330. Go 5.9 miles, and turn right onto County Road F17 W. Go 7.2 miles, and turn left onto Southwest Ave.; then go 0.4 mile, and turn right onto W. State St. Go 0.1 mile, and look for parking on the left.

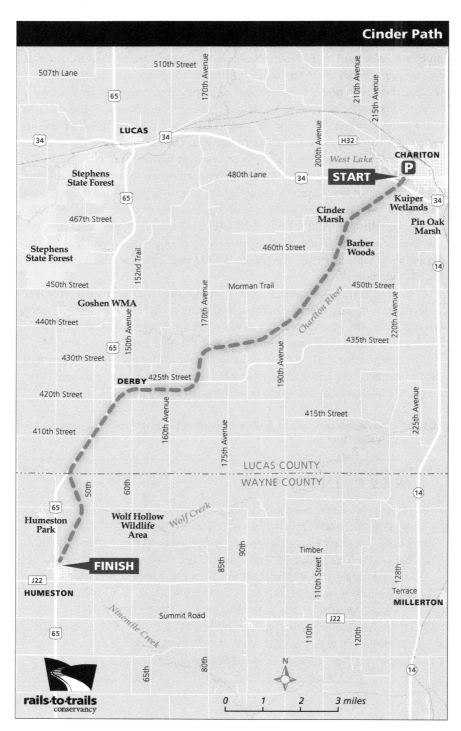

Cinder Path

The Cinder Path in southern Iowa is notable as the state's first rail-to-trail conversion. Following a shady route past farms and wetlands along the Chariton River between Chariton and Humeston for 13.5 miles, the crushed-stone and cinder surface shows its age in places. Grass covers the trail south of Derby, and the path can be challenging in rainy weather.

The trail follows a branch line of the Chicago, Burlington and Quincy Railroad built in 1872 that ran between Chariton and St. Joseph, Missouri. The railroad later became the Burlington Northern Railroad, which abandoned the railbed in 1974. The Lucas County Conservation Board bought the corridor that same year and established the trail.

Beginning in Chariton, you'll find a monument at the trailhead for community champion Dwaine Clanin, who played an integral role in the trail's conversion and development. Be sure to stock up on food and water before setting out, as services are rare along the Cinder Path. The trail

Several wooden bridges help mark the route of the Cinder Path.

Counties
Lucas, Wayne

Endpoints
Court Ave./US 34 Bus.
between Hy Vee Road
and S. 17th St. (Chariton)
to Fletcher St. between
N. Eaton Ave. and
N. Third St. (Humeston)

Mileage
13.5

Type
Rail-Trail

Roughness Index
2–3

Surface
Cinder, Crushed Stone

soon takes you into woods along the river—offering the sight of a flock of pelicans or waterfowl whenever an opening in the tree buffer arises. You'll frequently pass benches and resting areas along the way, although they show lots of wear.

Several wooden bridges mark the route to Derby, including a covered bridge about 6 miles from Chariton. You're also likely to see deer, rabbits, and other wildlife along the trail.

The trail enters Derby in 9.7 miles and runs through town streets for 0.3 mile. Turn left onto Front Street when you arrive, follow it to the right onto Derby Avenue, and then turn right onto Vine Street at a T-junction. The trail reappears on the left in what looks to be an empty grassy lot; the groomed section and a small sign will help you identify the path.

Riding a bike with fat tires or walking is the best way to explore past Derby, as the trail is grass-covered and can be soggy. Entering Wayne County, you'll notice that gates bar horses and all-terrain vehicles at the rural road crossings.

You'll arrive in Humeston 5.6 miles after leaving Derby. The Humeston Union Depot and Museum, one block south of the trailhead at 422 North Eaton Avenue, is worth a visit for railroad buffs. The town served as a junction for the Chicago, Burlington and Quincy and the Missouri, Iowa and Nebraska Railroads beginning in 1880. The two railroads agreed to build the combined depot, which was completed in 1883. A wooden water tower across the street is said to be the last remaining such structure in Iowa.

CONTACT: lucascountytourism.org/parks

DIRECTIONS

To reach the northern trailhead in Chariton from I-35, take Exit 33 onto US 34 E toward Osceola. Go 24.7 miles, turn left onto Bus. US 34/Court Ave., and then immediately bear right onto Bus. US 34. Go 0.3 mile, and look for trailhead parking on the right.

To reach the trailhead in Derby from I-35, take Exit 33 onto US 34 E toward Osceola. Go 17.7 miles, and merge with US 65 in Lucas; then go 0.6 mile, and turn right onto US 65. Go 6.8 miles, and turn left onto Front St. Go 0.8 mile, and look for on-street parking in the vicinity of Front and Broad Streets. After parking, backtrack 0.1 mile to Vine St., turn left, and look for the trail on the right.

To reach the southern trailhead in Humeston from I-35, take Exit 22 east onto E. Line St./120th St. Go 1.8 miles, and turn right onto US 69; then go 1 mile and turn left onto County Road J22. Go 14 miles, and turn left onto S. Front St./US 65; then go 0.6 mile, and turn right onto Fletcher St. Go 0.1 mile to find the trail on the left. On-street parking is available in the vicinity of Fletcher St. and N. Eaton Ave. and at the Humeston Union Depot and Museum at 422 N. Eaton Ave.

While Greater Des Moines is flush with multiuse trails, one of the paved pathways running through the suburb of Clive really stands out. Offering a string of trailside parks and fun twists and turns as it follows scenic Walnut Creek, the Clive Greenbelt Trail is a popular local amenity that's worth a visit if you're traveling in the area.

On the west end of the trail in Lions Park, you'll have the opportunity to easily connect to two other trails: the Heart of the Warrior Trail, which heads 3 miles west, and the well-loved Raccoon River Valley Trail, which travels west and then north for more than 80 miles to Jefferson. From the park, you'll travel east on the Greenbelt, winding through pleasant suburban neighborhoods.

A note of caution if you start on this end of the trail: Once you arrive at Northwest 142nd Street (after 1.6 miles of riding), things get a little confusing; you'll be riding on

Though never far from civilization, the Clive Greenbelt Trail gives the sensation of being away from it all.

Counties
Dallas, Polk

Endpoints
Lions Park at Wildwood Drive and NW 159th St./ Heart of the Warrior Trail (Clive) to 73rd St./Walnut Creek Trail (Windsor Heights)

Mileage
7.9

Type
Greenway/Non-Rail-Trail

Roughness Index
1

Surface
Asphalt, Concrete

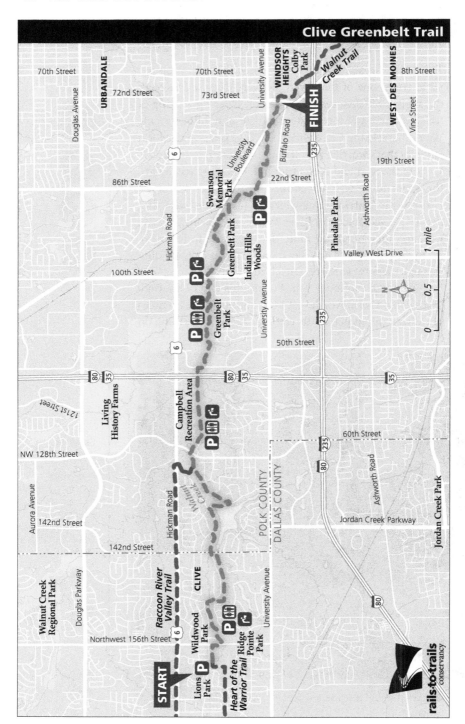

Clive Greenbelt Trail

what feels like a sidewalk along Lakeview Drive and then on an on-road stretch on Country Club Boulevard, all while following occasional bike route signs, but not much else in terms of way-finding. Locals may appreciate the trail's presence here, but visitors may prefer to start farther east at the Campbell Recreation Area, where the trail immediately dives into woodlands, and you can easily see why it's called the "Greenbelt."

The lush border of trees gives you the feeling of being away from it all, while restaurants, stores, and other businesses are positioned within easy reach of the pathway. Numerous well-marked spurs spin off the trail to destinations such as parks, city hall, and the public library. The Greenbelt's popularity in the community is easily felt here, as dog walkers, joggers, bikers, families, and outdoor enthusiasts of all sorts can be found on the trail.

If your excursion takes place between May and September, you're in for another visual treat. The Art Along the Trail exhibit is held annually on the Greenbelt during this time frame with six sculptures made by Iowans showcased trailside. At the end of the event, one of the pieces is selected for a permanent place in the city's public art collection.

On its east end, the trail enters Windsor Heights and seamlessly connects to the Walnut Creek Trail, which in turn ties into other trails in the expansive regional network.

CONTACT: cityofclive.com/government/parks-and-recreation/parks-trails

DIRECTIONS

The west end of the trail is located in Clive at Lions Park (15880 Wildwood Drive), though for a seamless trail experience a better place to begin a trip is at the Campbell Recreation Area (12385 Woodlands Pkwy.). To reach the recreation area from I-35 northbound, take Exit 125 for US 6/Hickman Road. Turn left (west) onto US 6/Hickman Road, and go 0.8 mile. Turn left at NW 128th St., and travel south for a half mile. Turn left onto Woodlands Parkway, and follow it for 0.3 mile until you see the entrance to the Campbell Recreation Area on your left. The endpoint at Lions Park is 3 miles west along the trail.

The closest parking for the eastern end of the trail is located at the trailhead in Clive. To reach the trailhead from I-235, take Exit 2 for 22nd St. toward W. Des Moines/Clive, and go 0.6 mile. Continue onto NW 86th St., and go 0.2 mile. Turn left into the trailhead; parking is available to your right at the end of the short access road. The endpoint is located 1.3 miles east along the trail at 73rd St. in Windsor Heights (also the northwestern endpoint for the Walnut Creek Trail).

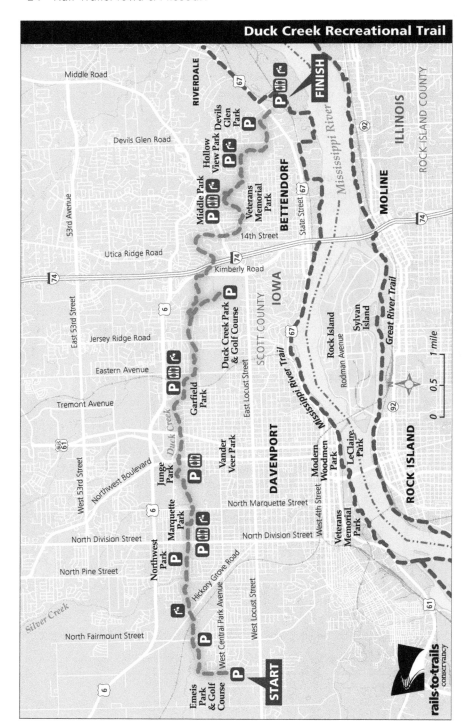

The Duck Creek Recreational Trail, also known as Duck Creek Parkway Trail, traverses three riverfront cities in the Quad Cities region of eastern Iowa, offering residents the opportunity for a peaceful stroll, bike ride, or stress-free commute. While the mighty Mississippi River, just south, is never within sight, the trail offers its own peaceful water views, as the path's namesake is never more than a stone's throw away.

Start at Emeis Park on the western side of Davenport, the largest of the five Quad Cities—an oxymoronic misnomer. The sprawling park offers several ballfields, a golf course, and a well-marked trailhead. Leaving the park, the trail quickly joins Duck Creek, which is slightly more narrow here than at the eastern end of the trail. As you proceed east, you'll realize why this trail is so popular with locals: spurs provide access to almost every nearby neighborhood street, and more than a handful of city parks line the route.

County
Scott

Endpoints
Emeis Park at W. Central Park Ave. and Emeis Park Ave. (Davenport) to S. Kensington St. and State St./US 67 (Riverdale)

Mileage
13.5

Type
Greenway/Non-Rail-Trail

Roughness Index
1

Surface
Asphalt

The Duck Creek Recreational Trail's namesake is never more than a stone's throw away.

Junge Park and Garfield Park are two of the larger parks; both offer ballfields, picnic tables, and playgrounds. Several trail bridges over Duck Creek provide opportunities for gazing at the wildlife below, including ducks, which firmly understand this is their creek. After the trail passes safely under I-74, the creek—wider at this point as it cuts through Bettendorf—and trail follow each other even more closely, guaranteeing additional waterfowl encounters. The only interruptions to this serenity are the occasional at-grade road crossings, although quick-to-respond trail signals and law-abiding vehicular traffic will have you moving on your way in no time.

At the trail's eastern end in the small manufacturing city of Riverdale, a massive aluminum plant looms ahead. Here a small trailhead welcomes trail users, although directional signage to a key connection is lacking; a short jaunt south on low-stress South Kensington Street leads to the Mississippi River Trail (see page 53), which provides easy access to the Mississippi River and downtown Davenport.

CONTACT: qcwildplaces.com/node/130

DIRECTIONS

To access the western trailhead at Emeis Park in Davenport from I-280, take Exit 4, and head east on Locust St. After 1.7 miles, turn left onto Emeis Park Ave., and proceed to the end of the street. Look for parking on your left at the Emeis Golf Course, immediately adjacent to the trail's starting point.

To access the eastern trailhead in Riverdale from I-74 heading north, take Exit 4, and turn right (east) onto State St./US 67. After 2 miles, turn right onto S. Kensington St. A small, paved parking lot and trailhead are located immediately to your right after the intersection.

estled in the suburbs of Des Moines and traveling through the towns of Ankeny, Berwick, Pleasant Hill, and Altoona, the Gay Lea Wilson Trail is named for a local advocate who first conceived of a network of trails in eastern Polk County in the 1980s. Eventually, the trail will link several central Iowa communities and open spaces over a 35-mile course. Currently, the trail connects East Des Moines with Ankeny to the north and Pleasant Hill and Altoona to the northeast.

County
Polk

Endpoints
SE Oralabor Road/
Oralabor Gateway Trail
between Windover
Drive and NE 19th Lane
(Ankeny) to First St.
E and Eighth Ave. SE
(Altoona); Scott Ave.
and E. Oakwood Drive
(Des Moines)

Mileage
20.9 miles

Type
Rail-with-Trail

Roughness Index
1

Surface
Asphalt, Concrete, Dirt

Eventually, the Gay Lea Wilson Trail will connect multiple central Iowa communities along a 35-mile course.

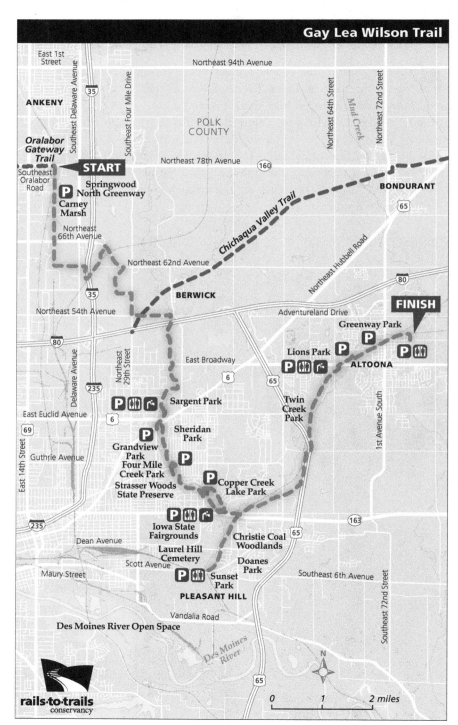

Gay Lea Wilson Trail

At the northern trailhead in Ankeny, trail users have the option of connecting with the Oralabor Gateway Trail and heading west for 5 miles to just past Northwest Toni Drive, where the Oralabor Gateway Trail connects with the Neal Smith Trail (see page 56) and creates a seamless off-road route to Saylorville Lake.

Beginning at the northern trailhead, the Gay Lea Wilson Trail winds southwardly along rural roads and through suburban neighborhoods that offer many access points for locals. Residents use the trail to walk or bike to recreation facilities, the library, and other town amenities. Benches are strategically placed for taking breaks, spotting birds, and snapping photos of Iowa wildflowers.

After a horizontal stretch heading east along Northeast 54th Avenue—an intersection for the 27-mile Chichaqua Valley Trail (see page 15), which travels northeast to Baxter—the trail meets with Fourmile Creek and then heads south under I-80. Here, the trail is enveloped by dense, quiet woodland as it follows the creek to Pleasant Hill and Copper Creek Lake, which the trail circles. At the south end of the lake, you'll find a large picnic area, a playground, water fountains, restrooms, and parking. Bring a picnic lunch and enjoy the scenery, or head east, where restaurants are in abundance.

From this central hub of the trail, a segment accessible at North Pleasant Hill Boulevard runs south for 1.5 miles along Fourmile Creek and an active rail corridor to Scott Avenue in East Des Moines. A less-than-0.5-mile trek west along hilly Fairview Drive/Dean Avenue (intersecting this segment's midpoint, before Scott Avenue) leads to the sprawling Iowa State Fairgrounds.

At North Pleasant Hill Boulevard, you can also take the trail northeast approximately 4 miles to the heart of Altoona. Much of this portion of the trail's route parallels an active railroad line.

A planned southern extension of the popular High Trestle Trail will eventually meet the Gay Lea Wilson Trail at Southeast Oralabor Road in Ankeny. Both trails are part of the Central Iowa Trail Network, which, when complete, will run about 110 miles and will also include the Neal Smith Trail, Heart of Iowa Nature Trail, and Chichaqua Valley Trail.

Note: While the very flat trail surface is composed of asphalt and concrete for a majority of its length, there are a few portions of dirt surface in heavily wooded areas.

CONTACT: www.polkcountyiowa.gov/conservation/parks-trails
/11-gay-lea-wilson-trail

The trail winds through many suburban neighborhoods, making it convenient for commuting and recreation.

DIRECTIONS

The nearest parking lot to the northwestern trailhead is located a half mile south along the trail at SE 54th St. in Ankeny. To reach the parking lot from I-80, take Exit 135 for IA 415 N/ NW Second St., and go 3 miles. Turn right (east) onto NE 66th Ave., and go 0.7 mile. Turn left onto NE 14th St., go 0.6 mile, and turn right onto NE 70th Ave., which turns into SE 54th St. Turn left into the parking area just after passing the marsh and crossing over the trail. The endpoint is located about 0.5 mile north along the trail at SE Oralabor Road, also the eastern endpoint for the Oralabor Gateway Trail.

To reach the nearest parking lot to the northeastern trailhead at the intersection of First Ave. S and First St. E from I-80, take Exit 143 toward Altoona. Turn right onto First Ave. N, and go 1 mile. Turn left onto First St. E immediately after the railroad tracks, and turn left into the parking lot. The endpoint is located about 0.6 mile east along the trail at Eighth Ave. SE.

To reach the southernmost trailhead in Pleasant Hill from I-235, take Exit 10A for IA 163 E/E. University Ave. Head east for 1.4 miles, and turn right onto E. 30th St. Go approximately 1.1 miles, and turn left onto Scott Ave. Go 1.4 miles, and turn left onto E. Oakwood Drive. Make an immediate left into the trailhead parking lot.

Built on a former section of the Chicago Great Western Railroad (built in 1893), the Great Western Trail spans 16.5 miles from just outside of urban Des Moines southward to Martensdale.

Begin your journey in the southern section of Water Works Park, just north of George Flagg Parkway, where you'll find parking, restrooms, and several nearby bars and restaurants that are popular with cyclists and other trail users.

Leaving the outskirts of Des Moines, you'll come across a major street crossing at IA 28, and then cut through the Willow Creek Golf Course before reaching a second major crossing at IA 5. A short time later, you'll reach Orilla, after which the trail empties into rural territory with cornfields and woods; here the ride is quiet and peaceful.

Counties
Polk, Warren

Endpoints
Water Works Park at Gray's Lake Road north of George Flagg Pkwy. (Des Moines) to Inwood St. and Iowa Ave. (Martensdale)

Mileage
16.5

Type
Rail-Trail

Roughness Index
1

Surface
Asphalt, Concrete

The Great Western Trail offers rural serenity just outside of urban Des Moines.

Great Western Trail

About 3 miles southwest of Orilla, the trail passes through the tiny town of Cumming, where there are restrooms and parking available, as well as a bar and a distillery.

The route then becomes completely rural, with open fields quickly transitioning to shady woodlands that feel extremely remote—particularly during the work week. Highlights along this stretch include a historic railcar and panoramic views of the North River. The trail finishes at a large trailhead in Martensdale, where restrooms and parking are available.

Note: Near the northern end of the Great Western Trail, an expansion of Veterans Parkway will shift the route of the trail slightly. Construction of the new trail section paralleling the new roadway between IA 5 and the city of Cumming is expected to be completed in 2019.

CONTACT: **warrenccb.org/parks-habitats/greatwesterntrail**

DIRECTIONS

To reach the northern endpoint and parking in Des Moines from I-235, take Exit 7 toward Martin Luther King Jr. Pkwy. (7A if heading west and 7B if heading east), and head south on Martin Luther King Jr. Pkwy. for about 1.1 miles. Continue south on Fleur Drive for 0.8 mile. Turn right onto George Flagg Pkwy. and go just under 2 miles. Turn left into the parking lot, just across from the Izaak Walton League building. The endpoint is located 0.1 mile north along the trail at Water Works Park.

To reach the southern trailhead in Martensdale from I-35, take Exit 56 for IA 92 toward Indianola/Winterset. Head east on IA 92 for 1.3 miles, and turn north onto 30th Ave. Go 0.3 mile, and turn right onto Inwood St. Go 0.3 mile, and turn left into the trailhead parking lot.

Heart of Iowa Nature Trail

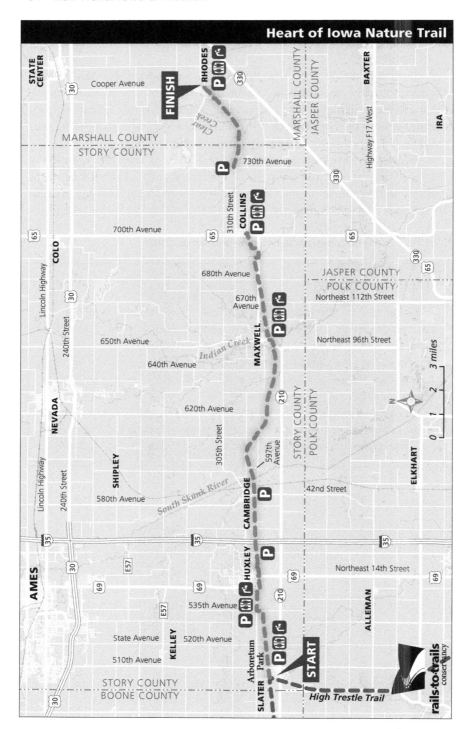

The Heart of Iowa Nature Trail traverses classic Iowa farmland along the former route of the Chicago, Milwaukee, St. Paul & Pacific Railroad, also known as the Milwaukee Road. The trail transitions from smooth crushed limestone in the west to a rougher grass and dirt surface in the east, with a couple of on-road detours. While a hybrid bike is a minimum requirement for cyclists, those riding fatter tires might find the trip more enjoyable.

The trail connects the former depot towns of Slater, Huxley, Cambridge, Maxwell, Collins, and Rhodes. Most provide services to trail users. They originally served as stops on the Milwaukee Road's east-west railroad link

Classic Iowa farmland helps to frame the Heart of Iowa Nature Trail.

Counties
Marshall, Story

Endpoints
First Ave. N and Greene St. near High Trestle Trail (Slater) to Railway St. and Second Ave. (Collins) and 730th Ave. between 310th St. and 305th St. (Collins) to E. Jefferson St. between N. Jackson St. and E. Walnut St. (Rhodes)

Mileage
25.8

Type
Rail-Trail

Roughness Index
2–3

Surface
Asphalt, Crushed Stone, Grass

between Chicago and Omaha until the company abandoned the railbed in 1982. The conservation boards of Story and Marshall Counties have maintained the trail since 2003.

Beginning at the junction with the paved High Trestle Trail on First Avenue in Slater, you'll follow signs for the Heart of Iowa Nature Trail through town to a trailhead park on the eastern outskirts.

After heading across open farmland for a few miles, you'll encounter a permanent on-road detour for 1.3 miles that turns left onto 535th Avenue, right onto West First Street, and then right onto South Fifth Avenue.

Back on the trail, the trek continues as before, with a crushed-stone surface and brief stretches of asphalt at road intersections. After skirting the southern edge of Cambridge, the trail crosses the South Skunk River on a newer trail bridge with overlooks. You'll likely notice the crushed-stone surface start to lose its firmness; hoof marks point to heavy equestrian use.

Upon the approach to Maxwell, you'll cross a new trail bridge over Indian Creek. Turn right onto Army Post Road at the old concrete bridge abutment and then left onto IA 210/Main Street to enter town on this 0.6-mile detour. A right turn onto Broad Street regains the trail at the Legion Park soccer fields.

The route east out of Maxwell is much the same, although you'll lose some tree cover along this stretch. The trail segment ends in Collins at a trailhead with ample parking on Railway Street. The farming community celebrates vintage tractors the second Sunday of September for the Go CAPOOT (Collins Area People on Old Tractors) Tour.

There is no sanctioned detour to a 4.4-mile-long orphaned trail segment east of Collins that features one of the trail's highlights, the massive Hoy Bridge. Heading east from 730th Avenue, the trail crosses Clear Creek on the 212-foot-long, 60-foot-high reinforced-concrete arch bridge built in 1912. A path down the embankment offers a creekside view. You'll arrive in Rhodes in another mile, where the trail abruptly ends, awaiting a future extension east.

Note: Story County allows hunting and trapping in November, December, and January between 520th and 535th Avenues, between 597th and 640th Avenues, and between 670th and 680th Avenues.

CONTACT: **co.marshall.ia.us/departments/conservation /conservation-and-recreation-areas/heart-of-iowa-nature-trail**

DIRECTIONS

To reach trailhead parking in Slater from I-35, take Exit 102 onto westbound IA 210. Go 5.4 miles, and turn right onto Linn St. (County Road R38). Go 0.5 mile, and look for the TRAILHEAD PARK AND ARBORETUM sign on the right. Turn left onto the path in the back of the parking lot, and go about 200 feet to the trail. The western trailhead is 0.5 mile to the left along the trail at First Ave. N and Greene St.; a right turn heads toward Collins.

To reach the trailhead in Collins from I-35, take Exit 102 onto eastbound IA 210. Go 9.5 miles, and turn right in Maxwell to remain on IA 210/Fifth St. Go 4.7 miles, and turn left onto US 65/First Ave. Go 0.6 mile, and turn right onto First St. in Collins, and then go about 400 feet and turn right onto Second Ave. Trailhead parking is straight ahead after crossing Railway St. in one block.

To reach parking at the western end of the Rhodes section from I-35, take Exit 102 onto eastbound IA 210. Go 9.5 miles, and turn right in Maxwell to remain on IA 210/Fifth St. Go 4.7 miles, and turn left onto US 65/First Ave. Go 1 mile, and turn right onto 310th St. in Collins; then go 3 miles, and turn left onto 730th Ave. Look for a small parking turnout in 0.1 mile on the right.

To reach trailhead parking in Rhodes from I-35, take Exit 102 onto eastbound IA 210. Go 9.5 miles, and turn right in Maxwell to remain on IA 210/Fifth St. Go 4.7 miles, and turn left onto US 65/First Ave. Go 1 mile, and turn right onto 310th St. in Collins; then go 3 miles, and turn left onto 730th Ave. Go 1.8 miles, and turn right onto 295th St. Go 3.3 miles, and turn right onto S. Main St. in Rhodes. Go 0.1 mile, and look for parking on the left at the junction with W. Kimball St. The endpoint is located less than a half mile northwest at E. Jefferson St.

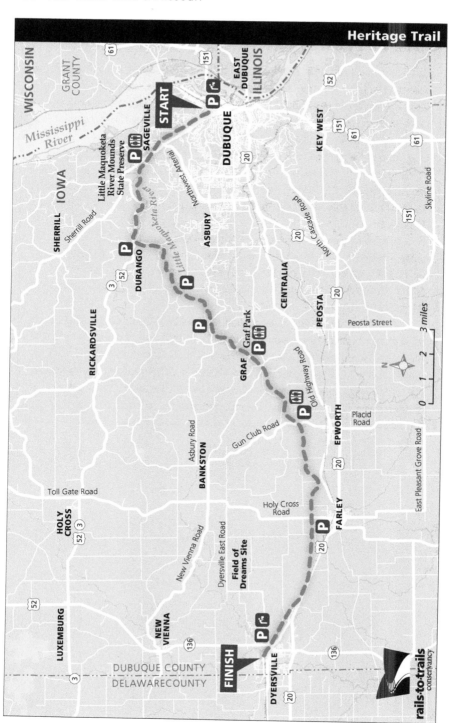

The Heritage Trail rolls along like a dream for nearly 30 miles from the Mississippi River town of Dubuque to Dyersville, home of the movie set for *Field of Dreams*. Along the way it passes through the deeply carved valley of the Little Maquoketa River, historical sites, and a handful of small farming and former mining communities.

The trail follows the corridor of the Chicago Great Western Railroad built in the 1880s to link Chicago, Minneapolis, Omaha, and Kansas City. Merging with the Chicago & Northwestern Railroad in 1968, the company determined that many of the 32 bridges and trestles were unsafe for railroad traffic and abandoned the line in 1981. The Dubuque County Conservation Board acquired the railbed and created the crushed-limestone trail in the mid-1980s. Several of those historic railroad bridges have since been replaced after severe flooding.

A historic trestle pays homage to the trail's old railroad days.

County
Dubuque

Endpoints
E. 22nd St. at Elm St. and Kniest St. (Dubuque) to Beltline Road between Fourth Ave. NE and 11th St. SE (Dyersville)

Mileage
29.4

Type
Rail-Trail

Roughness Index
1

Surface
Asphalt, Crushed Stone

The Heritage Trail passes through a handful of small farming communities along its route.

Beginning in Dubuque, you'll start your trek a couple of miles north of the historic riverfront that's home to an excursion riverboat and the National Mississippi River Museum & Aquarium. You'll head north out of Dubuque on pavement through an older residential and commercial area to a greenway that leads to the Heritage Pond trailhead and interpretive site in Sageville.

By now the trail is crushed limestone as you pass about 2 miles south of the Little Maquoketa River Mounds State Preserve on the way to Durango, where canoeists like to launch flow trips down the river to the Mississippi. Lead mining was an early industry in this area, and some landmarks still carry the name "furnace" referring to lead smelters.

The trail continues through the river drainage for nearly 8 miles to the town of Graf. Fossil hunters come here to look for remains of tiny prehistoric sea creatures in the limestone cliffs along the river and old railroad cuts. Endangered plant species, such as prairie dock and Leonard's skipper, also can be found in the trailside vegetation. A picnic shelter and restrooms are available in Graf, but there's no drinking water.

You'll gain a gentle slope as you climb out of the river bottoms toward Epworth and Farley. Both are less than 2 miles south of the trail and provide cafés and other services for travelers. The Centennial Ballpark north of Epworth has restrooms and drinking water.

The final 6 miles to Dyersville is all farmland, where you can be forgiven for expecting to see old-time baseball players emerging from the cornfields. Movie producers chose a farm 3.5 miles northeast of the Dyersville trailhead as the setting for *Field of Dreams*. The farm has since become a tourist attraction.

Note: Trail users age 12 and older must carry a trail pass costing $2.10 per day or $10.25 per year ($5.50 for individuals age 63 and older). An annual family pass is $25.50. Passes are available at area sporting goods and bicycle stores, at trailside businesses, and at trailhead parking lots.

CONTACT: **dubuquecounty.org/conservation/heritage-trail**

DIRECTIONS

To reach the eastern trailhead in Dubuque from US 20/Dodge St., turn left to head north on Locust St. toward US 151/US 52 N. Go 0.1 mile, and turn right onto IA 946 N.; then go 0.1 mile, and turn left onto US 151/US 52 N. After 0.5 mile, exit onto Ninth St. toward 11th St./US 52, and then go 0.2 mile to turn left onto Ninth St./Kerper Blvd. In about 200 feet, turn right onto Elm St. Go 0.7 mile, and turn right onto Rhomberg Ave. Go 0.1 mile, and turn left onto Kniest St.; then go 0.2 mile and turn right onto 22nd St. The trailhead parking is immediately on the left. The endpoint is located about 0.5 mile northwest along the trail on Beltline Road just before the intersection with Fourth Ave. NE.

To reach the western trailhead in Dyersville from US 20, take Exit 294 toward Dyersville onto northbound IA 136/Ninth St. Go 1 mile, and turn right onto Beltline Road. Look for on-street and off-street parking immediately on your left. The trail starts on the right.

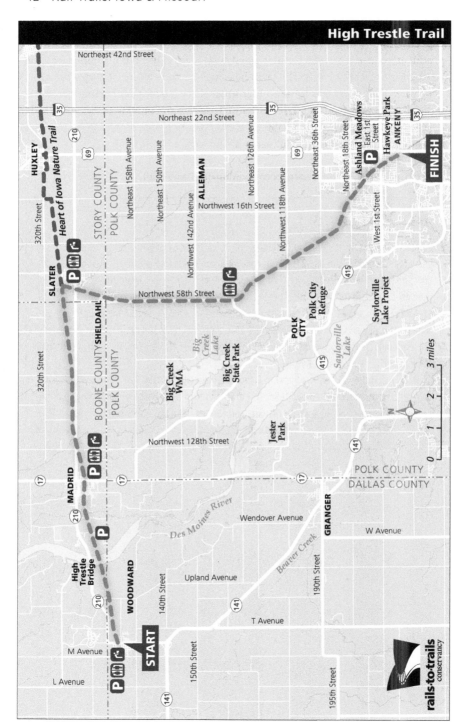

High Trestle Trail

The High Trestle Trail is one of the most pristine and highly trafficked trails in Iowa—even at night. The trail's popularity is largely due to its famous 130-foot-tall High Trestle Bridge, which boasts one of the most well-known rail-trail art installations in the country, *From Here to There*. Wrapped in 43 twisting, diamond-shaped steel ribs lined with LED lights, the bridge elicits the sensation of traveling down a mine shaft—a nod to the area's coal-mining history.

For individuals strictly interested in viewing the high trestle bridge (note that the trail is open 24 hours a day), there are two ideal entrance points. One, with lots of parking and a historic rail house, is located at the trail's northern endpoint in Woodward. The other—significantly closer than the Woodward access point—is a small parking area just off the trail outside of Madrid.

Counties
Boone, Dallas, Polk, Story

Endpoints
N. Main St./IA 210 and N. First St. (Woodward) to SW Ordnance Road and SW Railroad Ave. (Ankeny)

Mileage
25.6

Type
Rail-Trail

Roughness Index
1

Surface
Asphalt, Concrete

From Here to There on the High Trestle Trail is one of America's most famous rail-trail art installations.

If you're interested in traveling the entirety of the High Trestle Trail, the best place to start is at the west end in Woodward. Exhibits inside the former rail house explore the history of the disused line the trail now inhabits, and art and local signage pay homage to both the trail and the area's railroad days.

Heading east, the route takes you down a wide concrete path with typical Iowa farmland on either side. As you get closer to the Des Moines River, the landscape becomes more wooded and then opens up to the entrance of the trestle bridge, where you are welcomed by large concrete decorated columns—the beginnings of the art installation *From Here to There*.

Before entering the bridge, look to your left for a path that leads to an overlook; here you can see a breathtaking view of the trestle as it stretches out over the river. Entering the bridge itself, you'll be treated to another fantastic view as you are suspended higher and higher out over the river. The bridge's most notable feature is its collection of steel beams shaped and positioned to give the illusion of gliding movement if you're bike riding below them. At night, the beams are lined with glowing blue lights that create an otherworldly experience.

Past the bridge, the trail continues straight through forested areas and farmland before bending slightly and heading through the middle of the town of Madrid. Here, you'll find multiple spots for refreshment along the trail. Note the small tunnel decorated with trail- and railroad-themed paintings.

Leaving Madrid, you begin a long, straight stretch to Slater, passing by the backs of farmhouses, over small creeks, and—depending on the season—by expanses of wildflowers that grow in abundance along the trail. In Slater you'll also find a couple of spots with shelter, restrooms, and picnic tables for rest and respite. At Carol Street and First Avenue North, the trail makes a sharp right turn and heads southwest along the town's western edge. Here you can also head straight on First Avenue and then turn left onto the 25.8-mile Heart of Iowa Nature Trail (see page 34), which heads east to Rhodes. Back on the High Trestle Trail, you'll pass baseball diamonds, a pool, and a park to your right. You'll then travel through a short expanse of open land outside Slater before entering Sheldahl.

Continuing southward, you'll pass through more farmland and along blocks of crop fields, after which the trail follows Northwest 58th Street through flat Iowa cropland for several miles. Luckily there is a small oasis with a restroom, water, and a covered seating area just before the trail turns slightly east and heads toward Ankeny. From here, you'll travel through marshy-looking farms as you pass through a stretch just a couple of miles northeast of Saylorville Lake.

The trail runs diagonally through Ankeny—where farmland is replaced by neighborhoods and businesses—ending about halfway through the town.

CONTACT: inhf.org/what-we-do/protection/high-trestle-trail or
polkcountyiowa.gov/conservation/parks-trails/13-high-trestle-trail

DIRECTIONS

To reach the western trailhead in Woodward from Des Moines, head northwest on IA 141 and take Exit 138 for IA 210 E toward Woodward for 0.4 mile. Turn right (north) onto IA 210 E/ N. Main St., and go 1.7 miles. Turn right into the parking lot and trailhead after Railroad St.

To reach parking on the eastern side of the trestle bridge from IA 17 heading north, turn left onto E. First St. in Madrid, and go 0.5 mile. Turn right onto N. Locust St., and then make an immediate left onto W. North St. After 0.3 mile, continue on IA 210 W/334th Road. Go 1 mile, and turn left onto QF Lane. After 0.5 mile, look for parking on the right immediately after crossing over the trail.

The closest available parking for the eastern endpoint in Ankeny is a little less than 1 mile along the trail. To reach the parking lot from IA 415 N/SW State St., turn right onto W. First St., go 0.7 mile, and turn left onto NW Ash Drive. After 0.2 mile, turn left into the trailhead parking lot. Head southeast along the trail for just less than a mile to the endpoint at SW Railroad Ave. and SW Ordnance Road.

Depending on the season, wildflowers grow in abundance along the High Trestle Trail.

Iowa Great Lakes Trail

The Iowa Great Lakes resort on the northern border with Minnesota is a longtime destination for fishermen and vacationers who arrived from big cities by rail. Dickinson County employed two different former rail corridors, as well as streets and sidewalks, to create a 14.3-mile paved trail, known locally as the "Spine Trail," that can be used by a new generation of visitors to Spirit Lake, East and West Okoboji Lakes, and Upper and Lower Gar Lakes. There's a nearly limitless inventory of cafés and ice-cream stores along the route for food and refreshments.

The segment between the towns of Orleans and Spirit Lake follows a former corridor of the Iowa Northwestern Railroad, which abandoned the line in 2009. Historically

The Iowa Great Lakes Trail travels through the beautiful Lower Gar State Recreation Area.

County
Dickinson

Endpoints
125th St. and 253rd Ave. (Orleans) to 230th St. and 225th Ave. (Milford)

Mileage
14.3

Type
Rail-Trail

Roughness Index
1

Surface
Asphalt

This 1902 swing railroad bridge over West and East Okoboji Lakes connects Okoboji and Arnolds Park.

it operated as the Burlington, Cedar Rapids & Northern Railway, succeeded by the Chicago, Rock Island & Pacific Railroad. From Spirit Lake south through Milford, the trail runs on and off the old railbed of the Chicago, Milwaukee, St. Paul & Pacific Railroad (Milwaukee Road) that served the area from the 1890s. Parts of the trail date to 1992.

Beginning on the eastern shoreline of Spirit Lake, you'll head south between farm fields and lakeside homes for 1.5 miles to the town of Orleans. Throughout the Iowa Great Lakes Trail, your route switches from multidirectional trail to sidewalks to on-street bike lanes, so you'll have to watch for painted pavement arrows and bike signs.

Crossing a land bridge between Spirit Lake and East Okoboji Lake, the trail puts you along the water in Isthmus Park with picnicking and fishing areas. After crossing Hill Avenue, you'll zigzag through a wooded area, then pass cow pastures and crop fields before you enter the town of Spirit Lake. The trail here follows the former Iowa Northwestern Railroad right-of-way for less than 2 miles. The trail route then heads south alongside Peoria Avenue.

Turn left onto 20th Street and right onto Lincoln Avenue to find the trail again at 23rd Street, this time heading southwest on the former Milwaukee Road railbed. A side trail heads west alongside 175th Street toward Kenue Park Nature Center and a grand loop around West Okoboji Lake.

Following US 71/Okoboji Avenue past boat dealers and other marine businesses, turn left onto Gordon Drive and follow it right to cross the inlet linking East and West Okoboji Lakes on the 1902 swing railroad bridge to Arnolds Park.

This lakeside community is home to a 125-year-old lakefront amusement park of the same name, in addition to the Iowa Rock 'n' Roll Hall of Fame, which celebrates many of the acts that performed in local resorts over the years. Turning left onto Bascom Street and right onto Rohr Street takes you through a neighborhood to a trailhead on 195th Street. You'll enter a shady area along the Minnewashta Lake shoreline, cross a bridge, then return to a shady shore on Lower Gar Lake.

Leaving Lower Gar State Recreation Area, the route continues on a shared roadway along 202nd Street for 0.7 mile, and then left onto the trail. It continues 3.3 miles south through Milford, ending on 230th Street in Milford's Old Town, the center of the community in the late 1860s.

CONTACT: dickinsoncountytrails.com

DIRECTIONS

To reach parking for the northern trailhead in Orleans from I-35, take Exit 142 west toward Fort Dodge on US 20. Go 56.2 miles, and turn right onto IA 4; then go 45.9 miles and turn left, joining US 18 in Emmetsburg. Go 4.8 miles, and turn right onto IA 4; then go 20.1 miles, and turn left onto IA 9. Go 8.6 miles and join US 71. Go 4.4 miles, and turn right onto 255th Ave.; then go 1.1 miles, and turn left onto 140th St. Go 0.4 mile, and turn right onto 253rd Ave. Go 1 mile, and look for a gravel parking lot on the right. The endpoint is 0.5 mile north along the trail at 125th St. just east of 253rd Ave.

To reach parking for the southern trail endpoint in Milford from I-35, take Exit 142 west toward Fort Dodge on US 20. Go 56.2 miles, and turn right onto IA 4; then go 45.9 miles and turn left, joining US 18 in Emmetsburg. Go 15.6 miles, and turn right onto 310th Ave./County Road N14. Go 13.9 miles, and turn left onto 220th St./County Road A34. Go 8.7 miles, and look for a small parking lot on the right, just past Q Ave. on the left. The endpoint is 1.2 miles south along the trail at 230th St.

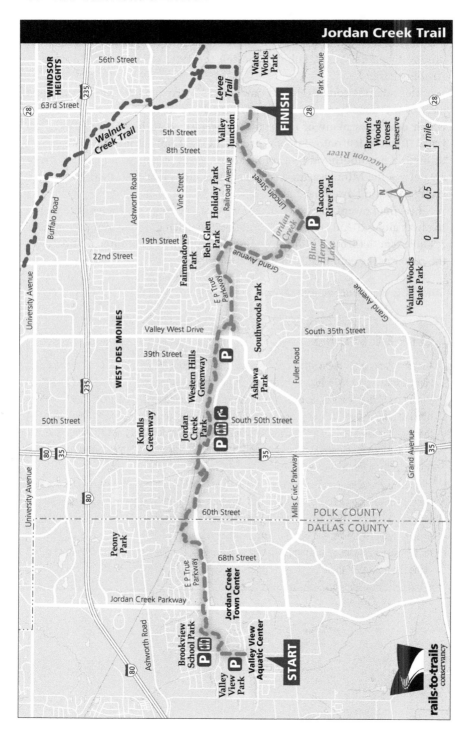

The Jordan Creek Trail is a pleasant suburban trail that connects neighborhoods with shopping and retail, schools, and recreational amenities. The trail gets its name from the Jordan Creek, which it follows—along with the EP True Parkway—for much of its route. There are many opportunities to hop on and off the trail to visit the Jordan Creek Town Center or enjoy dining in the many restaurants along the route. Way-finding signage makes it easy for users to know where they are headed, though the path isn't always marked as the Jordan Creek Trail. If you're unsure, simply follow signs for key landmarks, including Jordan Creek Park and Raccoon River Park.

Starting from the Valley View Aquatic Center parking lot, go to the intersection of 81st Street and Bridgewood Boulevard, and turn left onto 81st Street. Here, clear signage will direct you on how to stay on the trail.

For the next several miles, you'll follow the trail through suburban neighborhoods of West Des Moines and intersect with several shopping plazas that are rife with

The Jordan Creek Trail's many wooded sections make for a serene journey.

Counties
Dallas, Polk

Endpoints
Valley View Aquatic Center at 81st St. and Bridgewood Blvd. (West Des Moines) to SE First St./IA 28 just south of Railroad Ave. (Des Moines)

Mileage
8.6 miles

Type
Greenway/Non-Rail-Trail

Roughness Index
1

Surface
Concrete

retail opportunities. This section of trail overlaps with sidewalks in some places, so be sure to pay attention to trail markers and way-finding signage. Leaving the shopping area, you'll quickly return to peaceful neighborhood settings.

Many sections of the trail are wooded, offering a serene atmosphere that runs through two of West Des Moines' noteworthy parks—Jordan Creek Park and Raccoon River Park—the latter of which is considered the crown jewel of the West Des Moines park system. The sprawling 632-acre site is host to a variety of recreational amenities, including a large lake teeming with wildlife, a beach, a soccer complex, softball fields, a dog park, picnic shelters, and a trail around the lake.

At 39th Street, the trail passes the Des Moines Rugby Club, where parking and bike racks are available. The trail also passes historic Valley Junction (accessible by street; turn left onto IA 28/Southeast First Street and then left onto Maple Street), where visitors can enjoy a farmers market, shopping, dining, and live events. Shortly after passing Valley Junction, the trail dead-ends at IA 28/Southeast First Street. Here, you can choose to make a left onto Southeast First Street (also Southwest 63rd Street) and then a quick right onto the Levee Trail, which is not well marked but which connects you to the Walnut Creek Trail, a 2.4-mile pathway that runs through beautiful wooded parks.

The trail is part of the Central Iowa Trail Network, and at many points, trail users can access large network maps to identify and locate points of interest. Underpasses and tunnels make it easy for trail users to experience the route with little interruption from street traffic. Note that there are few public water fountains or permanent restrooms, and trailheads are not well marked. Plan to park at one of the public facilities at either end of the trail for the best experience.

CONTACT: wdm.iowa.gov/home/components/facilitydirectory
/facilitydirectory/26/1433

DIRECTIONS

To reach the Valley View Aquatic Center from I-80, take Exit 121 for Jordan Creek Parkway toward W. Des Moines, and head south for 1.7 miles. Turn right onto Bridgewood Blvd., go 0.5 mile, and turn right into the aquatic center, which has ample parking. Access points to the trail are located on 81st St. and marked with signage near the intersection.

The best place to park at the eastern end of the trail is at the Raccoon River Park Softball Complex, about 1.5 miles west. To reach the park from I-235, take Exit 4 for IA 28/63rd St. toward Windsor Heights. Turn right onto IA 28 S, and travel 1.7 miles. Turn right onto Lincoln St., and follow it for 1.6 miles. Turn left into the complex parking lot. The endpoint is located about 1.5 miles northeast along the trail at IA 28 just south of Railroad Ave.

The Mississippi River Trail in Scott County resembles the setting of a Mark Twain novel as it travels 13.5 miles along its namesake within sight of barges, riverboats, and marine-related businesses and activities. The paved trail (part of the larger 3,000-mile Mississippi River Trail system)—comprising riverfront sections in Bettendorf, East Davenport, Davenport, and Riverdale—also provides a platform to enjoy the riverfront parks, festivals, and music events in Davenport that have added a spark to the revitalization of the Quad Cities. In addition to connecting with the 13-mile Duck Creek Recreational Trail in Bettendorf, trail users can also link up with 60-mile Great River Trail, across the river in Illinois, which reaches Savanna.

A good place to begin your journey is in Riverdale—once famous for its dairy and large herd of Holsteins. While the eastern endpoint for the trail begins at Fenno Road and State Street, you'll find parking about 1.4 miles west, past the industrial area of Riverdale, at State Street and South Bellingham Street. The trailhead is tucked next to a large aluminum factory and an active rail line.

At Leach Park in Bettendorf, the Mississippi River Trail provides dazzling views of the waterway.

County
Scott

Endpoints
State St. and Fenno Road (Riverdale) to S. Concord St. where it meets with the local crossing to Credit Island Road on Credit Island (Davenport)

Mileage
13.5

Type
Greenway/Non-Rail-Trail

Roughness Index
1

Surface
Asphalt, Concrete

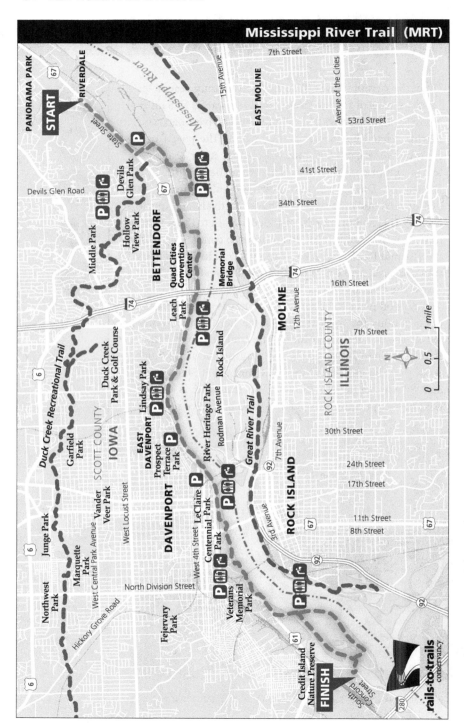

Mississippi River Trail (MRT)

In 0.4 mile the South Kensington Road crossing affords a connection to the Duck Creek Recreation Trail.

After winding past some waterfront facilities for river commerce for nearly 2.5 miles, the trail arrives at the shoreline in Bettendorf to reveal dazzling views of the Mississippi. Punctuated by frequent benches and the occasional sight-seeing pier, the smooth route takes you past the Quad Cities Waterfront Convention Center and the riverboat-style Isle Casino. Immediately following the casino is the grand sight of Memorial Bridge and Leach Park, which has both parking and a giant ship's wheel overlooking the waterfront. Across the river is the Rock Island Arsenal, the largest government-owned weapons maker and former prison for Confederate soldiers during the Civil War.

About 1.5 miles downriver you'll come to Art Park in lower Lindsay Park in the Village of East Davenport. The park serves as a companion site to a boat launch and yacht club. You'll find restrooms, a playground with whimsical arches, the bronze *Watching the Ferry* statue from a John Bloom lithograph, and a gazebo.

The greenway then takes you under the 1896 double-decker Arsenal Bridge and the much newer pedestrian Skybridge to downtown Davenport's waterfront at LeClaire Park. This is home to jazz and blues music festivals, as well as the colorful Rhythm City Casino and Ferris wheel. Just beyond is the Quad Cities River Bandits Minor League ballpark in Modern Woodmen Park and a large skate park in Centennial Park. Next you'll pass the meditative Veterans Memorial Park dedicated in 2011.

The trail passes through some trees along the river and onto Credit Island, an early trading post and site of a War of 1812 battle led by future US President Zachary Taylor. You can follow a 2.6-mile loop on low-traffic Credit Island Road around the island, or enjoy the natural preserve on a 1.6-mile nature trail. The trail crosses the water at the southwest end of the Island and ends at S. Concord St.

CONTACT: qcbc.org/maps/src/DavenportDuckCreekandRiverFront.pdf or qctrails.org/trails/trail/Mississippi-river-trail-io

DIRECTIONS

To reach the eastern trailhead in Riverdale from I-74, take Exit 4, and turn onto eastbound US 67/State St. Go 2.1 miles, and turn right onto S. Bellingham St. Look for parking on the right in 0.1 mile at the BIKE PATH PARKING ONLY sign. The endpoint is located about 1.4 miles northeast along the trail at State St. and Fenno Road.

To reach the western trailhead in Davenport from I-74, take Exit 4, and turn onto westbound US 67/Grant St. Go 5.6 miles (US 67/Grant St. becomes US 67/River Drive), and turn left onto Credit Island Road. Go 0.4 mile, and look for parking on the right. The endpoint is located about 1.6 miles southwest at S. Concord St.

Neal Smith Trail

Big Creek Lake

FINISH ▶

Northwest 58th Street

Northwest 44th Street

Northwest 142nd Avenue **ALLEMAN**

35

Big Creek State Park

415

Northwest 126th Avenue

Northwest 16th Street

69

POLK COUNTY

High Trestle Trail

Jester Park

POLK CITY

Saylorville Wildlife Refuge

415

Prairie Flower Recreation Area

Ankeny Boulevard

Northeast Delaware Avenue

Northwest 18th Street

Oak Grove Picnic Area

Cherry Glen Picnic Area

East 1st Street

Camp Dodge

Saylorville Lake

Northwest Beaver Dr

ANKENY

35

Oralabor Gateway Trail

141

Northwest 70th Avenue

Saylorville Dam

Cottonwood Recreation Area

69

SAYLORVILLE Northeast 66th Avenue

Sycamore Park

Northwest 100th Street

Merle Hay Road

JOHNSTON

Des Moines River

Northeast 54th Avenue

35 80

Trestle to Trestle Trail

35 80

Broadway Avenue

80

35

Northwest 86th Street

Aurora Avenue

Douglas Avenue

URBANDALE

6

Inter-Urban Trail

East Euclid Avenue

6

Riverview Park

69

235

Hickman Road

6

Prospect Park

Crocker Woods

Birdland Park

CLIVE

University Avenue

WINDSOR HEIGHTS

University Avenue

START ▶

DES MOINES

John Pat Dorrian Trail

rails·to·trails conservancy

N

0   1   2   3 miles

235

Part of an expansive trail network in the Greater Des Moines region, the 26-mile Neal Smith Trail rolls along the banks of the Des Moines River through the Ding Darling Greenway conservation area and makes its way through a variety of landscapes, including riverbanks, wildflower meadows, lakeshores, and dense forests. Plenty of benches offer ample opportunities for trail users to rest and enjoy the deer, rabbits, butterflies, and other critters active along the route.

The trail travels near several campsites and recreation areas with water fountains and restrooms, and parking is available at several points along the way. The trail also connects with several other trails, including the Oralabor Gateway Trail, the High Trestle Trail, and the Inter-Urban Trail. Portions of the trail are maintained by the U.S. Army Corps of Engineers, the Iowa Department of Natural

County
Polk

Endpoints
E. University Ave./John Pat Dorrian Trail just west of E. Sixth St. (Des Moines) to Big Creek State Park Beach and Marina (Polk City)

Mileage
26

Type
Greenway/Non-Rail-Trail

Roughness Index
1

Surface
Asphalt

The Neal Smith Trail features a variety of traditional Iowa landscapes.

Resources, and the City of Des Moines for year-round access, but note that only the city-maintained portion is plowed during the winter.

From the southern endpoint at East University Avenue—also the northern endpoint for the 3.4-mile John Pat Dorrian Trail—the Neal Smith Trail flows into Birdland Park along the Des Moines River. Portions of this section of the trail are prone to flooding, and trail users are advised to check the trail's website for closures and detours.

Just outside Birdland Park, the trail enters Riverview Park, where it intersects with the short Kiwanis Nature Island Trail and the McHenry Park Trail. At the north end of the park, you'll come to the eastern endpoint of the 1.3-mile Inter-Urban Trail, which cuts right and then makes a U to cross the Des Moines River, where you can also pick up the 3.7-mile Trestle to Trestle Trail to your right. The Neal Smith Trail continues through wildlife-rich forest and wetlands habitat following the contours of the Des Moines River.

About halfway along the route, you'll reach Saylorville Dam, holding back the eponymous lake on the Des Moines River. Saylorville Lake is host to a diverse range of recreational opportunities—including boating, fishing, camping, and more. The trail also passes a visitor center that offers public educational events, including guided rides along the Neal Smith Trail.

The trail continues along the lake's eastern shore through neighboring forests and some incredible wildflower prairie meadows, after which it shares a roadway through the Cherry Glen Picnic Area. Parking is available here during park hours, and the facility has restrooms and water access. The trail continues off-road at the north end of the picnic area on the far side of a large parking lot. A short distance farther, the pathway continues through the Prairie Flower Recreation Area campgrounds on a shared roadway; here, you'll have access to several restrooms and water fountains.

Nearing the end of your route, you'll enter Big Creek State Park, which has several picnic and recreational areas with parking, restrooms, docks, and lake access points. The trail ends at Big Creek Marina, which boasts a large playground, a sandy beach along the lakeshore, and ample parking.

CONTACT: www.mvr.usace.army.mil/missions/recreation/saylorville-lake
/recreation/trails

Big Creek Lake at Big Creek State Park near trail's end

DIRECTIONS

To reach parking at Birdland Park and Marina (near the southern endpoint of the trail) from I-235, take Exit 8B (E. Sixth St./Pennsylvania Ave.). Head north on Pennsylvania Ave. (left turn from northbound I-235, right turn from southbound I-235). In about 1.25 miles, the parking lot will be on your left. Enter from Pennsylvania Ave. or Birdland Drive. The endpoint is about 0.9 mile south along the trail at E. University Ave. Another parking lot is located by going 0.4 mile south on Pennsylvania Ave. and turning right (just before the intersection with Cleveland Ave.).

To reach the Big Creek Marina trailhead from downtown Des Moines, take I-235/I-35 northbound to Exit 96 (Elkhart/Polk City). Turn left onto NE 126th Ave., and follow for 1.6 miles. Turn right onto Ankeny Blvd., and go 2 miles. Turn left onto NE 142nd Ave. After around 7 miles, turn left onto NW Big Creek Drive, and then turn left at the intersection. The marina parking lot will be on your left.

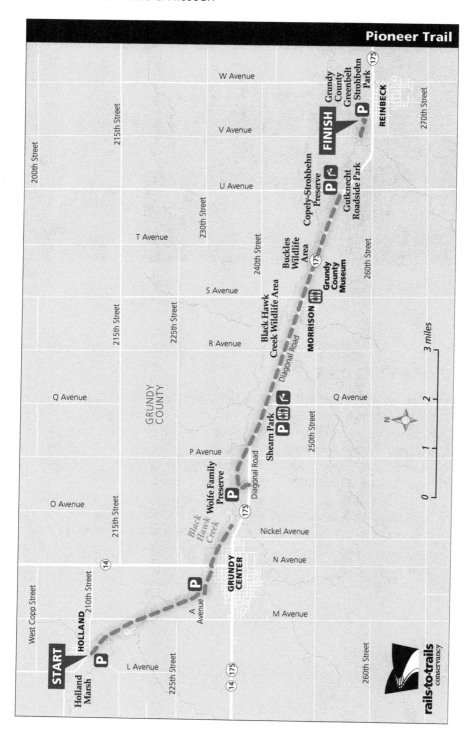

The nearly 12-mile Pioneer Trail—which gets its name from the early settlers in Grundy County—is built on a former rail line that once connected the towns of Holland and Reinbeck and the communities in between. The flat trail parallels Black Hawk Creek for most of its route as it showcases Iowa's natural conservation areas and farmland. It also features several commemorative plaques with tributes to trail supporters.

The complete trail, mostly tree-lined and shaded, consists of three sections separated by two gaps (around a mile each) on shared roadways. Horseback riding on the trail is allowed on the mowed grass parallel to the crushed-stone pathway.

From the northernmost endpoint in Holland, the trail begins at South Main Street, where there is a small parking area, and continues through a tree-lined area bordered by farmland. After the first 2.4 miles, the trail

Mostly tree lined and shaded, the Pioneer Trail consists of three separate segments of pathway.

County
Grundy

Endpoints
S. Main St. and Market St. (Holland) to N. Commercial St. near Grundy Ave./ IA 175 (Reinbeck)

Mileage
11.5 miles

Type
Rail-Trail

Roughness Index
2

Surface
Crushed stone

shares the roadway with A Avenue for about a half mile. The trail continues off-road on the east side of Fourth Street for another 0.8 mile and then reaches its first gap at 235th Street. You can continue on a shared roadway by turning right onto 235th Street and then left onto Diagonal Road.

The trail picks up again about a mile down the road at the entrance to the Wolfe Family Preserve (in the preserve's eastern end), where there is a small parking area.

The trail then enters a forested landscape before traveling back out into relatively open farmland as it parallels Diagonal Road. This section has three stops with picnic areas and restroom access: the C.E. Shearn Memorial Park (south side of Diagonal Road, approximately 1.8 miles in), the Grundy County Museum (south side of Diagonal Road at Second Street and Sycamore Street, approximately 4 miles in), and Gutknecht Roadside Park at U Avenue (approximately 5.5 miles in).

To reach the final section to Reinbeck, turn right onto U Avenue, and turn left onto Diagonal Road. The trail picks up just over a mile down the road on the east side of V Avenue and ends a quarter mile later at the Reinbeck Shooting Range, where limited parking is available.

CONTACT: **grundycounty.org/departments/conservation/trails/pioneer-trail**

DIRECTIONS

To reach the northwestern trailhead in Holland from Des Moines, take I-235 eastbound to Exit 137A to I-80 toward Davenport. In 4 miles, take Exit 142 to US 6/US 65 toward Altoona. Turn left onto NE Hubbell Ave., and continue for approximately 36 miles. Turn left onto Marsh Ave. to continue on IA 330 northbound for 13 miles. Turn left onto IA 14 northbound just after passing the Marshalltown Municipal Airport on your right. In about 16 miles, turn right to continue on IA 14/IA 175. In just over 6 miles, you'll reach the outskirts of Grundy Center. Turn left onto M Ave.; the Rose Hill Cemetery will be on your left. In 2.5 miles, turn left onto 210th St. Continue for just under 0.75 mile. Take a sharp left onto Market St. and then immediately turn right onto S. Main St. Turn left into the trailhead parking lot.

To reach the eastern trailhead in Reinbeck from Des Moines, take I-235 eastbound to Exit 137A to I-80 toward Davenport. In 4 miles, take Exit 142 to US 6/US 65 toward Altoona. Turn left onto NE Hubbell Ave., and continue for approximately 36 miles. Turn left onto Marsh Ave. to continue on IA 330 northbound for 13 miles. Turn left onto IA 14 northbound just after passing the Marshalltown Municipal Airport on your right. In 4 miles, turn right onto IA 96 eastbound, and go 14 miles. Turn left onto H Ave., and go 8.5 miles. Turn right onto IA 175 (Diagonal Road); after about 1.5 miles, turn left onto N. Commercial St. The roadway to the Reinbeck Shooting Range will be on your left across from a cluster of grain silos. The roadway leads to a small parking area at the end of the road.

The Prairie Farmer Recreational Trail follows part of the former Chicago, Milwaukee, St. Paul and Pacific Railroad corridor, which traces its origins as far back as 1866. Its history lives on in Cresco, where you can view a restored Milwaukee Road diesel engine at Beadle Park (on IA 9/Second Avenue, between Second Street and Elm Street) just over a half mile from the trailhead. Its history also lives on in Calmar, where a small interpretive loop explores signage from the Milwaukee Road era, and a historical rail depot (which houses an antiques store) greets travelers as they begin or end their journey.

The trail makes its way through some of the last native prairie habitat of the region, with spectacular wildflower meadows and scattered woodland areas lining the pathway. There are also ample opportunities to see wildlife and a wide variety of birds.

The southeast segment of the Prairie Farmer Trail ends in historic Calmar.

Counties
Howard, Winneshiek

Endpoints
IA 9/Second Ave. SE and Eighth St. E (Cresco) to Maryville St. and Lewis St. (Calmar)

Mileage
20

Type
Rail-Trail

Roughness Index
1

Surface
Asphalt

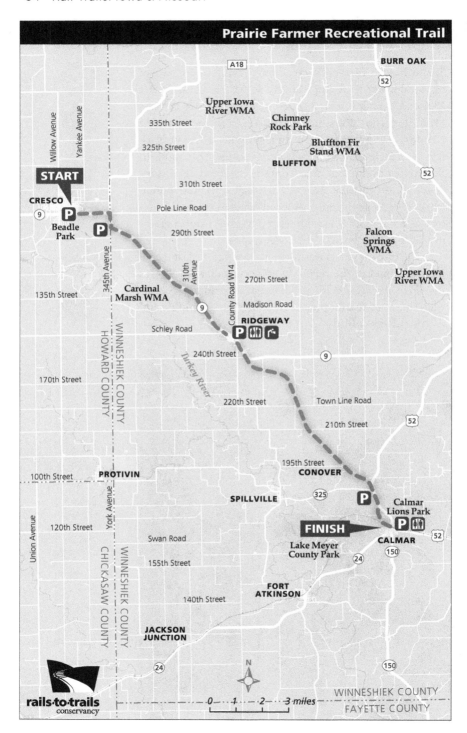

Prairie Farmer Recreational Trail

Start your journey in Cresco at Second Avenue SE/IA 9 and Eighth Street East, although be aware that there is limited parking at this trailhead. The path begins on a wide sidewalk and follows IA 9 to the edge of town. Note that additional parking is available at the access point at IA 9 and 345th Avenue, where the trail enters more of a tree-lined corridor paralleling the highway.

A little more than 8 miles in, you'll reach the town of Ridgeway, where the trail shares a roadway through town. Sharrows are marked on the road but are a bit faded. Turn right onto Short Street and then left onto County Street Road. When you reach the edge of town, take a sharp left onto 295th Street where it meets with County Road W14. The short gravel road will take you back to the off-road portion of the trail at Ridgeway Roadside Park, where you'll find a sheltered picnic area, a playground, water, parking, and pit toilets.

The trail continues through a mostly wooded corridor. Just after the town of Conover, there's a small interpretive loop with historical signage from the Milwaukee Road era. The loop provides a nice shaded rest area under the forested canopy.

As you enter the town of Calmar, you're greeted on your right side with the portion of the railway that remains in use. The trail passes through a small park that is home to the Winneshiek County Freedom Rock—a memorial to honor veterans and first responders. The memorial is a project of artist Ray Sorensen, who paints patriotic scenes on the stones and hopes to decorate one for each of Iowa's counties. The park has plenty of parking, a gazebo, and benches.

The trail ends at the restored train depot in historic Calmar. Inside the depot you'll find a range of displays on the city's railroad history as well as an antiques shop. A public restroom is available on the south side of the building, and plenty of parking is available at the depot and on the streets in town.

CONTACT: co.howard.ia.us/offices/conservation/recreation
.htm#prairie_farmer_recreational_trail

DIRECTIONS

To reach the northern trailhead in Cresco from Waterloo, take US 63 northbound for about 60 miles, and turn right onto IA 9. Go 9 miles to Cresco, and turn left into the trailhead parking lot just past Eighth St. E. Farther along IA 9, you can reach another small parking area at 345th Ave., after the highway makes a bend to the right.

To reach the southern trailhead in Calmar from Waterloo, take US 63 northbound for 34 miles. Turn right onto 240th St., go 6.5 miles, and turn left onto Roanoke Ave. After 4 miles, turn right onto IA 24, and go about 20 miles. In Calmar, turn right onto Main St., go three blocks, and turn left onto Maryville St. The Calmar train depot will be on your left, just past the railroad tracks. Parking is available on the north side of the station, and street parking is available throughout the town. The trail begins 0.2 mile east at Maryville St.

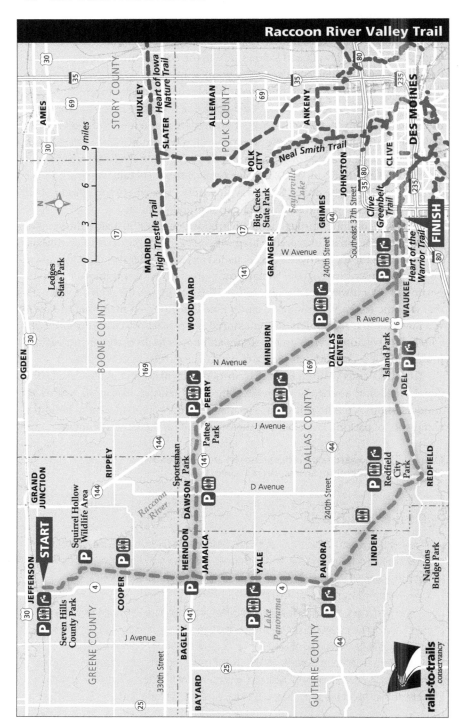

On the western outskirts of Des Moines, the Raccoon River Valley Trail offers a quintessential central Iowa experience. Over its nearly 90-mile span, you'll traverse wooded, prairie, and agricultural landscapes. The route forms a loop through several rural communities with a long tail coming off the loop on its northern end that heads to Jefferson, and another tail on its southern end that rolls out toward Des Moines.

The Raccoon River Valley Trail runs along a former railroad right-of-way that was first built in the 1870s to carry rail traffic between Des Moines and the Great Lakes region. Fully paved and with a level grade typical of a rail-trail, it's an easy walk or ride, though you may wish to conquer the trail over the course of multiple days due to its size. Note that using the trail requires a $2 daily fee for

The 600-foot-long trestle bridge over the North Raccoon River outside the town of Jefferson

Counties
Dallas, Greene, Guthrie, Polk

Endpoints
E. Lincolnway St. just east of S. Cedar St. (Jefferson) to Hickman Road west of NW 128th St. (Clive)

Mileage
88.1

Type
Rail-Trail

Roughness Index
1

Surface
Asphalt, Concrete

A section of the Raccoon River Valley Trail through Winkleman Switch

individuals age 18 and older. All proceeds go to the conservation boards in the counties through which the trail passes, and the money is used for trail maintenance and improvements. Look for the payment drop boxes at the trailheads.

At the northern trailhead in Jefferson, you'll be greeted by a former Milwaukee Road depot painted a cheerful yellow. Although the building is open only for special occasions, ample parking is available here, and a drinking fountain can be found outside to fill up your water bottles for the journey. From the depot, you'll head south past country homes for a few blocks until the trail dives under a shady tree canopy. The trail opens up to farmland as it approaches the old railroad town of Cooper at mile 7. Come in the summer, and you'll see a plethora of grasshoppers darting across the pathway. A highlight of this section is the 600-foot-long trestle bridge over the North Raccoon River.

From Cooper, it's 5 miles to Herndon, where you'll come to your first trail junction. This is where the loop portion of the route begins. Turn left to travel east to the towns of Jamaica, Dawson, and Perry, or continue your southward momentum to the towns of Yale and Panora.

If you choose the eastern leg, you'll pedal through peaceful, picturesque terrain: farm fields and wildflower meadows interspersed with copses of trees. To either side of the trail, the brushy embankments are also bustling with birds. After 7 miles, you'll see another depot (circa 1889) sitting trailside in Dawson. Peek inside at the displays of railroad history and the old baggage room. Here, you'll also find restrooms and drinking water.

In another 6 miles, you'll come to Perry, one of the larger towns along the route. The community truly embraces the trail, and in the windows of many businesses are signs welcoming trail visitors. You'll pass a self-service bicycle-repair station as you enter the town, which also has a refurbished depot with restrooms, drinking water, and a covered picnic table. Restaurants and lodging are plentiful here.

From Perry, your trajectory turns southeast as you roll through the small farming town of Minburn and then Dallas Center a few miles later. In Waukee, you arrive at your second trail juncture. You can finish your day's journey by taking the short trail segment east along US 6 (Hickman Road) to the trail's end in Clive. If you're not done riding yet, pass under US 6 to seamlessly pick up the Clive Greenbelt Trail (see page 21), which will take you through the West Des Moines suburbs.

To stay on the Raccoon River Valley Trail, in Waukee, pivot west to continue on the trail's loop toward Adel. From Adel, you'll pedal through Redfield, Linden (named for its many linden trees), and Panora in relatively quick succession. At Panora, you'll pass a lovely trailside garden and a covered shelter with railroad signage and a small section of track. The trail turns north here, and you'll have 6 miles to go before reaching Yale, where you'll pass by a massive grain silo, as well as a city park with restrooms and water.

You're on the homestretch now with 5 miles to go before reaching Herndon, the site of your first trail junction. Upon arrival, you'll have experienced the entirety of the Raccoon River Valley Trail.

CONTACT: raccoonrivervalleytrail.org

DIRECTIONS

At the northern end of the trail in Jefferson, parking is available at the restored depot. From downtown Des Moines, take I-35 north for about 28 miles to Exit 111B for US 30 W (toward Ames). Head west about 41 miles to Jefferson, and turn left onto IA 4 (N. Elm St.). Go 1.3 miles, and turn left onto E. Lincolnway St. Travel seven blocks east to the parking lot, which is to your right just after you pass the depot.

In Waukee, on the southern end of the trail, you can park at the intersection of US 6 (Hickman Road) and Ashworth Drive/N. 10th St. From I-80 westbound, take Exit 117 for Waukee. Turn right (north) onto County Road R22 (which becomes Sixth St.), and go 3.5 miles to Ashworth Drive. Turn left onto Ashworth Drive, and follow it for a half mile to the trail parking lot, which is located to your right and left just after you cross US 6. The trail's eastern endpoint is located about 4.8 miles east. After passing Woodlands Pkwy., the trail heads south underneath US 6/Hickman Road to its starting point just west of NW 128th St. and just north of Pineview Drive.

Rock Island Old Stone Arch Nature Trail

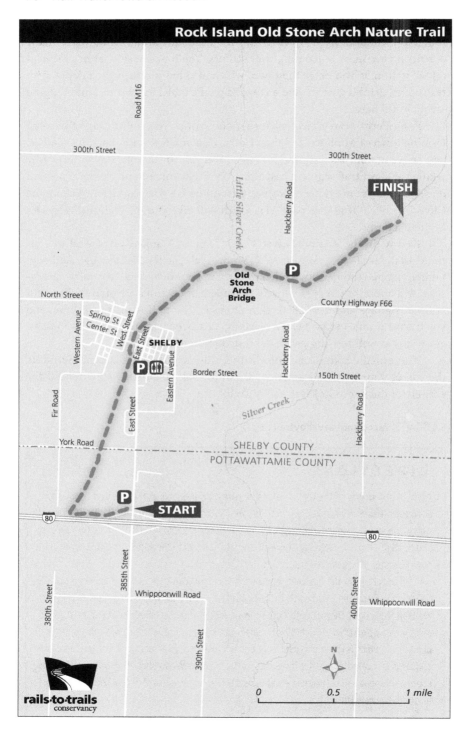

The Rock Island Old Stone Arch Nature Trail travels 4 miles along an asphalt path atop a former railbed once owned by the Chicago, Rock Island & Pacific Railroad. Starting near an I-80 on-ramp, the trail rolls through the town of Shelby before ending at a bridge across Silver Creek.

The old stone arch bridge that gives the trail its name dates from 1883. Listed on the National Register of Historic Places, the 35-foot stone structure is said to be the first railroad structure built in Shelby County.

Beginning at Exit 34 on I-80, the trail provides a great opportunity to get off the highway and stretch your legs. It is ideal for families, runners, and cyclists looking for a short, easy, and beautiful ride.

Facing a restaurant on the northwest corner of the interchange, you'll head left (west) toward a small landscaped park with benches marking the trail entrance.

An expansive view of the Rock Island Old Stone Arch Nature Trail looking east from Hackberry Road

Counties
Pottawattamie, Shelby

Endpoints
385th St. between I-80 westbound on-ramp and County Road L34/ York Road to east of Hackberry Road at Silver Creek (Shelby)

Mileage
4

Type
Rail-Trail

Roughness Index
1

Surface
Asphalt, Crushed Stone

Gravel for the first hundred yards may not be suitable for wheelchair users. The rest of the trail is paved, passing through a green corridor of farmed fields and restored wetlands.

You'll follow the trail west for 0.4 mile before heading north 1 mile to Shelby, where the rail line arrived in 1868 on its way to Council Bluffs. A restored train depot with restrooms greets visitors arriving by trail, and an old Burlington Northern caboose stands nearby. You can find restaurants in town, and parking is available.

In the summer, keep your eyes peeled for purple martins, the largest North American swallow. They congregate in birdhouses built along the trail, making this a great place for casual bird-watchers. Residents mounted some 50 bird-houses in the community, earning Shelby a designation as the Purple Martin Capital of Iowa for its natural mosquito eradication program.

You'll find the stone arch bridge 1.1 miles past the train depot. The trail ends at Silver Creek in another 1.1 miles at another old railroad bridge.

CONTACT: shelbyia.com/attractions.asp

DIRECTIONS

To reach the southern trailhead from I-80, take Exit 34 onto 385th St. toward Shelby. Take the first left into a restaurant and gas station, and find parking on the left. The trail begins just past the small landscaped park.

To reach trailhead parking in Shelby from I-80, take Exit 34 onto 385th St. toward Shelby. Go 1.1 miles, and turn right onto Station St. Parking is straight ahead at the restored depot.

To reach the northern trailhead from I-80, take Exit 34 onto 385th St. toward Shelby. Go 1.2 miles, and turn right onto Spring St. Go 1.1 miles as Spring St. becomes County Road F66, and turn left onto Hackberry Road. Go 0.2 mile, and find parking on the left. The endpoint is located 0.9 mile northeast along the trail (on the eastern side of Silver Creek).

The Sauk Rail Trail offers some of the best riding in rural, west-central Iowa. The paved 33-mile trail is capped at either end by a state park and offers a diverse mix of views and experiences in between. Friendly small towns every few miles add comfort and convenience, while frequent nods to the corridor's railroad past add historical interest.

Start at the trail's north end in Lake View to be welcomed by a unique sculpture over the trail entrance: an arch made of bicycles. As you face the trail, you can swing your head to the left to see Black Hawk Lake just two blocks down. Black Hawk Lake State Park is nestled against its shoreline; the 86-acre site offers numerous amenities for camping, hiking, hunting, fishing, canoeing and kayaking, and horseback riding.

A trail user fee of $2 per day is required for individuals age 18 and older; look for the self-service pay box at the

A unique arch greets visitors to the Sauk Rail Trail at its northern endpoint in Lake View.

Counties
Carroll, Sac

Endpoints
Third St. between Vine
St. and McClure St.
(Lake View) to Swan
Lake State Park (Carroll)

Mileage
33.2

Type
Rail-Trail

Roughness Index
1

Surface
Asphalt, Concrete

trailhead. Heading south, you're soon enveloped by trees as you travel through a wildlife area and, just a mile later, alongside Black Hawk Marsh.

After about 13 miles of riding, you'll reach Breda, home to about 500 residents. Be sure to have a look inside the community's restored 1905 depot, which sits trailside and includes memorabilia from the Chicago & Northwestern Railroad.

South of Breda, the vista opens up to expansive farm fields. Windmills dot the horizon, and you'll likely see cows out in the pastures. Keep your eyes open for deer and rabbits; you might catch a fleeting glimpse of them as they dive into the underbrush along the trail. You'll also pass under an old wooden trestle bridge on your way to Carroll. As you enter the city, the bucolic flavor of the trail gives way to a suburban atmosphere.

Most of the trail thus far will have been fairly level, but as you approach the trail's end at Swan Lake State Park, you'll encounter a few hills. Plunk yourself down on a bench to enjoy some well-earned rest and lake views, or loop around the lake for a 3.8-mile ride. If you're planning to stay overnight, tent and RV camping are available within the park, a 510-acre multiuse area offering a range of outdoor activities and amenities.

CONTACT: sauk-trail.com

DIRECTIONS

To reach the northern trailhead in Lake View from US 71 northbound, turn left (west) onto 330th St./IA 175. After 4.2 miles, turn left onto Third St. Go 0.5 mile (road turns into Crescent Park Drive), continue as the road turns into Lake St., and then take a slight left to stay on Lake St. Turn right onto Third St., and go 1.5 blocks. Parking and the trailhead with its distinctive arch are located on your left.

At the southern end of the trail, parking is available in Swan Lake State Park (22676 Swan Lake Drive). From US 71 northbound, turn right onto 220th St. After 1.4 miles, turn right onto the park access road, and look for parking on your right.

Summerset Trail

The Summerset Trail links the two central Iowa communities of Indianola and Carlisle, both of which have embraced the trail, including providing helpful signs at each end with clear directions for trail users to reach local amenities. Between the two towns, there is a lot of peaceful nothingness, with the dominant farm views ranging from an occasional peek through the surrounding tree cover to wide-open vistas.

In Indianola, the Summerset Trail proceeds north from a well-appointed trailhead, while the connecting McVay Trail travels more than a mile southeast past the local high school to community softball fields. This easy access means that you're likely to encounter cross-country teams and other area youth as you head north out of town on the longer trail to Carlisle.

Peacefulness characterizes the route of the Summerset Trail between Indianola and Carlisle.

County
Warren

Endpoints
McVay Trail at N. Fifth St. north of E. Clinton Ave. (Indianola) to 165th Place and IA 5 (Carlisle)

Mileage
12

Type
Rail-Trail

Roughness Index
1

Surface
Asphalt

As you first travel north out of Indianola, you'll encounter a few road crossings without signals where patience is required. (Take some comfort in knowing that it is these frequent crossings that provide easy access to the trail for residents of the many nearby neighborhoods.) After East Hillcrest Avenue, the scene quickly turns rural in nature, and you won't encounter another road—and sometimes another person—for miles. Enjoy the surrounding tree cover; you'll lose the shade roughly halfway through the route, shortly after you pass an entrance to Banner Lakes at Summerset State Park. Consider taking a detour into the park to enjoy the water views.

Losing the envelope of trees is a worthy trade for the spectacular scenery that is gained thereafter. Farmland seems to stretch endlessly in both directions, and in the summer, the trail is lined spectacularly by bright yellow wildflowers. The trail is joined by a parallel road for the final couple of miles into Carlisle, and an adjacent subdivision means that the trail becomes more frequented by families with young kids. In Carlisle, end at the large trailhead on the right, or briefly head west along IA 5 and then north along South First Street to reach the community's charming downtown.

CONTACT: mycountyparks.com/county/warren/park/summerset-trail.aspx

DIRECTIONS

To reach the southern trailhead in Indianola from I-35, take Exit 56 for IA 92 W, and head east on IA 92 for 11.8 miles. Turn left onto S. Jefferson Way, go 0.2 mile, and then turn right onto E. Ashland Ave. and go 0.2 mile. Turn left onto N. Fifth St., go 0.2 mile, and turn left into the trailhead parking lot (restrooms and drinking fountains are available here).

To reach the northern trailhead in Carlisle from I-35, take Exit 68 for IA 5 toward West Des Moines/Norwalk, and head south on IA 5 for 11.1 miles. Continue onto IA 5 S/US 65 N for 1.8 miles, and then take Exit 72 for IA 5 S toward Carlisle for 0.5 mile. Continue onto IA 5 S, and go 2.3 more miles. Turn right onto 165th Place, and turn right into the trailhead parking lot.

The Three Rivers Trail runs for nearly 40 miles from the small community of Rolfe—named after the early English settler who married Pocahontas—to just west of Eagle Grove. The mostly rural trail is named appropriately for the three rivers it crosses, including the West Fork and East Fork of the Des Moines River and the west branch of the Boone River, and is ideal for those seeking peace and solitude.

Starting in Rolfe at the small trailhead and parking area, you'll head southeast on a flat route with little to no grade. For those wishing to bike, the town of Rolfe offers a bike-share program; look for the bike station at the J.B. Wilcox Shelter and Picnic Area at the trailhead. During the first 16.5 miles to Humboldt, you'll head over the West Fork Des Moines River and through prairie and farmland, crossing many railroad trestles along the

River crossings are common along the route of the Three Rivers Trail.

Counties
Humboldt, Pocahontas, Wright

Endpoints
300th Ave. and Railroad St. (Rolfe) to Calhoun Ave. between 250th St. and 255th St. (Eagle Grove)

Mileage
39.9

Type
Rail-Trail

Roughness Index
1

Surface
Sand, Dirt, Grass

Three Rivers Trail

way. Just before the trail crosses Pilot Creek Road, look for a sizable historical marker denoting the site of a battle between the Winnebago and Sioux Indians in 1854 to control the area's abundant resources. Here, you'll also find a parking lot, a pit toilet, and a picnic shelter.

Be sure you stock up on water and snacks for your journey, as there are no food amenities or public water fountains along this stretch.

After Jerry Hatcher Road in Humboldt, you can curve left onto a separate, 6-mile spur trail that extends north to open farmland (note that there's no outlet at the spur's end) or south to Frank A. Gotch State Park, a 67-acre campsite, and the confluence of the East and West Forks of the Des Moines River. Back on the main trail in Humboldt, the trail continues southeast to Dakota City and passes the Humboldt County Historical Museum—a complex of historical buildings reflecting early life in the county—located at the southern end of the Dakota City Memorial Park & Campground. Most prominent is the 13-room mill farmhouse built in 1879. You'll then cross the East Fork Des Moines River before continuing to more rural settings once again.

The trail continues through trees and farmland, crosses over the last of its namesakes, the Boone River, and ends abruptly about 1.5 miles west of the small town of Eagle Grove, at Calhoun Avenue. There are no amenities at this end of the trail, and trail users who wish to enter town must take local roads.

CONTACT: **humboldtcountyia.org/county-park/three-rivers-trail**

DIRECTIONS

To reach the western trailhead in Rolfe from US 169 heading north, turn left onto 270th St., and go 11 miles. Continue onto 570th St. for 5 miles, and then turn right onto 290th Ave. Go 10.1 miles, and turn right onto 470th St. After 1 mile, turn left onto 300th Ave. Go 0.3 mile, and look for the small trailhead on the right (just before the road curves left and becomes Railroad St.).

To reach parking south of Humboldt from Fort Dodge on US 169 heading north, turn right onto 120th St.; go 2 miles, and turn left onto National Ave. After 2 miles, continue onto 100th St./280th St. for 0.2 mile, and then continue onto Lone Tree Road for 3.5 miles. Turn left into the parking area where the trail intersects the road.

To reach parking at the eastern endpoint from Webster City on IA 17, take IA 17 N for 13.5 miles. Turn left onto W. Broadway St., go 0.9 mile, and continue onto 270th St. Turn right onto Calhoun Ave. After 1.3 miles, look for a small parking area to your left, where the trail begins.

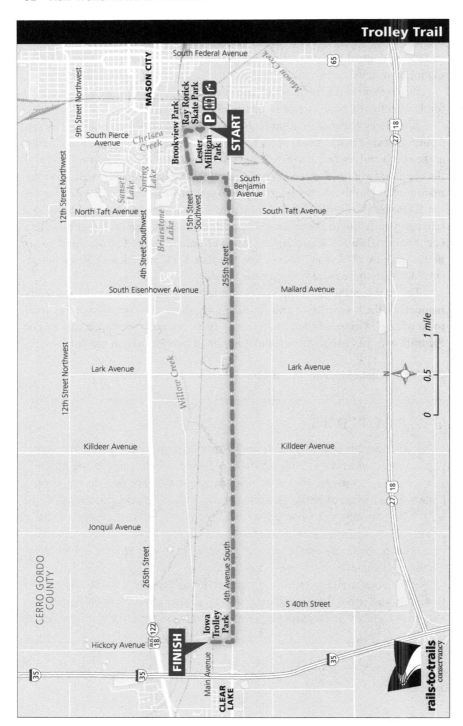

The best place to begin the Trolley Trail is in Mason City in Ray Rorick Skate Park, located adjacent to the 81-acre Lester Milligan Park, which has two fishing and swimming ponds, hiking and biking trails, a playground, water, and restrooms, as well as a railroad that weaves into town. On the other side of the skate park's ample parking lot is an entrance for the Trolley Trail—which is part of the small trail network that circles the park.

Heading north and then west on the Trolley Trail, you will be surrounded by—and will then head over—a cluster of small ponds; note the clear water of the largest of the ponds, named Big Blue, which is suitable for swimming and fishing. There is a small parking area and dock on the pond, as well as a tiny beach area.

As you travel west, you'll follow along railroad tracks briefly before turning left (south) onto South Benjamin

County
Cerro Gordo

Endpoints
Ray Rorick Skate Park north of 15th St. SW and east of S. Pierce Ave. (Mason City) to Main Ave. west of N. 35th St. (Clear Lake)

Mileage
7.5

Type:
Greenway/Rail-with-trail

Roughness Index
1

Surface
Asphalt, Concrete

Iowa Trolley Park makes for an interesting endpoint for rail line history buffs.

Avenue; this road takes you to where the formally labeled "Trolley Trail" begins— to your right—just above 19th Street Southwest.

The trail jogs along an industrial park with warehouses and manufacturing facilities, passes a high school, and then jumps to the other side of the road at South Taft Avenue.

As you travel farther away from the center of Mason City, the surroundings get slightly more rural. You'll notice cornfields on either side, as well as an old trolley line running on the opposite side of the road.

Approaching the western endpoint in Clear Lake, the trolley tracks veer right (north) toward the Iowa Trolley Park, where a small museum is open to the public on weekends (10 a.m.–4 p.m. from Memorial Day to Labor Day). You'll continue on the trail along the road (now Fourth Avenue South) for about a half block, after which the trail cuts right and heads north into an open, grassy area to the trolley park (on your right), ending at Main Avenue. The trolley park makes for an interesting endpoint for rail-line history enthusiasts.

CONTACT: traveliowa.com/aspx/trails.aspx?id=32

DIRECTIONS

To reach the eastern trailhead at Ray Rorick Skate Park from I-35, take Exit 190 for US 18 E/ IA 27 E toward Mason City. Continue onto IA 27 S/US 18 E for 3.6 miles, and take Exit 183 toward Mallard Ave. Turn left onto Mallard Ave., go 1.5 miles, and continue on S. Eisenhower Ave. for 0.5 mile. Turn right onto 19th St. SW/255th St., and go 2 miles. Turn left onto S. Pierce Ave., go 0.2 mile, and turn right onto 15th St. SW. After 0.2 mile, turn left into the park before you reach the railroad tracks. Look for a large parking lot ahead and to the right, inside the park. There is no dedicated parking lot at the western end of the trail.

The Trout Run Trail provides an experience unique to any other in Iowa, with a hilly landscape that reminds trail users of the meteorite that struck the area long ago. The trail actually loops all the way around the town of Decorah, and the northern portion follows along the Upper Iowa River.

Starting from the west side of Decorah off Fifth Avenue and Pulpit Rock Road, the trail follows along the water, curves right, and then heads left into two campgrounds; note the signage as you wind through. At the south end of the campgrounds, you'll cross a small bridge and then have the option to continue east or cut a sharp right and head south.

Heading south, a brief switchback climb cuts through the rocky hillside and up to a small overlook with rock walls on either side of the trail. The route then heads back

A switchback along the Trout Run Trail in Decorah

County
Winneshiek

Endpoints
Fifth Ave. and Riverview Dr. to Walmart lot at IA 9 and County Road A52/Old Stage Road (Decorah)

Mileage
11

Type
Greenway/Non-Rail-Trail

Roughness Index
1

Surface
Asphalt, Concrete

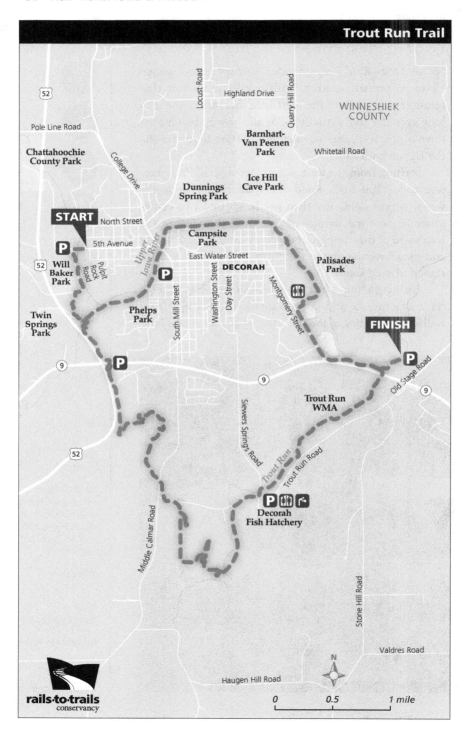

downhill along the highway (to your right) and then comes to a large intersection, where a newly finished trail overpass bridge glides you to the other side; here, depending on the season, you'll be greeted by an abundance of wildflowers. Parking and a detailed trail map are also available.

The trail heads south and outside of town and then takes a sharp left turn—wiggling you through cornfields and up and down switchbacks. Continuing south, you'll come to another sharp series of switchbacks through more cornfields at the southernmost section of trail; take some time to enjoy the beautiful and abundant hills that grace the route.

The trail curves northward through farms along Trout Creek and heads right past the Decorah Fish Hatchery and then left across Trout Run Road and over the creek. From here, you'll follow the creek northeast until you reach the Trout Run Access Area and the Upper Iowa River, where the trail cuts northwestward. As you make your way around the northern loop segment along the river, the route passes several art installations, including a silver archway shaped like a swimming fish, and a trestle bridge picnic area.

Along the way, you're likely to come across cows, wildflowers, and hiking paths venturing off the trail. After you pass a large school and sports fields, the trail and river veer left and head southward to where the loop began. Note that this part of the trail is prone to flooding.

Ahead a short way is Phelps Park with a playground and lots of green grassy spots. You'll then come to a straight strip of trail that takes you along a rocky hill face—part of Decorah's originality—and by a couple of sculptures before connecting back to the campgrounds.

CONTACT: **troutruntrail.com**

DIRECTIONS

To reach the northwest trailhead and parking from US 52 heading north toward Decorah, turn right onto Pulpit Rock Road for 0.6 mile. Turn right into the parking lot, which is located just before you reach Fifth Ave. The endpoint is located 0.1 mile east on Fifth Ave. just before the intersection with Riverview Drive to the north.

To reach the eastern trailhead/Walmart from IA 9, head northeast (a right turn if you're heading west, a left turn if you're heading east) onto Old Stage Road, and then turn left into the Walmart parking lot. The trail connection is at the western corner of the lot near the Upper Iowa River.

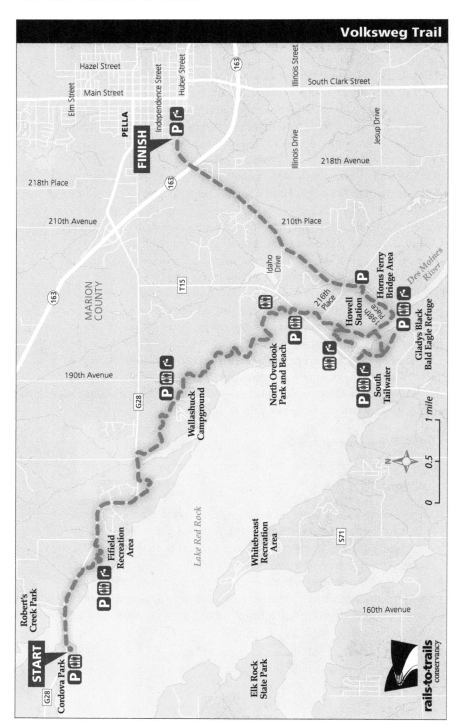

Volksweg Trail

Who says Iowa doesn't have hills?! The winding route of the Volksweg Trail sticks mainly to the rolling hills and scenic viewpoints from Lake Red Rock all the way to the town of Pella. Dutch immigrants settled this lovely section of Iowa in the mid-19th century, which explains how the Volksweg Trail, Dutch for "people's path," got its name.

Normally a 12.5-mile trek, the steepest 3.7-mile section of trail that plunges to the base of the dam on the Des Moines River is closed until sometime in 2018 while crews work on a hydroelectric project. A 0.9-mile detour on local roads reconnects to the final leg into Pella.

Beginning at the trailhead on the west side of the bridge across Robert's Creek, you'll head east alongside County Road G28 on a trail separated from the road for 3 miles that passes through the Fifield Recreation Area.

Scenic Lake Red Rock is a prominent feature of the 12.5-mile Volksweg Trail.

County
Marion

Endpoints
County Road G28 at Fillmore Dr. in Cordova Park to University St. at W. Fifth St. (Pella)

Mileage
12.5

Type
Greenway/Non-Rail-Trail

Roughness Index
1

Surface
Asphalt

Leaving the road after crossing Wallingslock Creek, you head into some woods as you skirt the northern edge of Wallashuck Campground. If you are thirsty, you can grab a drink at the Wallashuck trailhead, which also has restrooms and parking available to your right.

About 2.5 crooked miles down the trail from the Wallashuck trailhead, you will pass by a well-equipped playground right before the landscape opens up to North Overlook Recreation Area park and beach. Many visitor amenities, such as restrooms, picnic tables, and drinking fountains, can be found here.

To go around a trail closure and continue to Pella, you can take a detour left onto County Road T15 (0.3 mile) and right onto Idaho Drive (0.6 mile). Idaho Drive reconnects with the trail across the street from a gas station. This portion of trail is uneven, with cracked pavement that may be difficult for some users.

From here you can follow the remaining 2 miles on the trail along Idaho Drive all the way to the Volksweg Water Plant Trailhead, located at West Fifth Street and University Street. If your timing is right, you may arrive for Tulip Time festival in early May. Otherwise, you may want to visit the Dutch-themed town center about a mile away via University Street and Main Street. You'll find a historical village, a Dutch windmill, and plentiful coffee shops and bakeries.

CONTACT: americantrails.org/NRTDatabase/trailPhotos/3845_167_2012
VolkswegTrailMapbothsides.pdf or redrockhydroproject.com
/images/uploads/RRHP_Camground_Closures__RRHP_Facts
_FINAL_2015-0423.pdf

DIRECTIONS

To reach the western trailhead at Cordova Park from I-80, take Exit 155 onto southbound IA 117 toward Colfax. Go 1.1 miles, and turn left onto State St.; then go 0.7 mile, and turn right to stay on IA 117/S. League Road. Go 5.3 miles, and turn left onto E. Second St./IA 163. Go 1.9 miles, and turn left to stay on IA 163, and then go 8.2 miles to Exit 29, and turn right onto IA 14. Go 5.1 miles, and turn left onto County Road G28. Go 3 miles, and turn right into the parking lot.

To reach the eastern trailhead in Pella from I-80, take Exit 155 onto southbound IA 117 toward Colfax. Go 1.1 miles and turn left onto State St.; then go 0.7 mile and turn right to stay on IA 117/S. League Road. Go 5.3 miles and turn left onto E. Second St./IA 163. Go 1.9 miles and turn left to stay on IA 163. Go 21.3 miles, take Exit 40, and turn left onto Washington St. Go 1.5 miles, and turn right onto W. Third St.; then go 0.5 mile, and turn right onto University St. In 0.2 mile, turn left into the parking lot.

A Rails-to-Trails Conservancy Hall of Fame rail-trail, the Wabash Trace Nature Trail earns its title—providing an amazing trip through the rural forests and countryside of southwest Iowa. The trail takes you on a 62.6-mile journey from Council Bluffs (just outside of Omaha, Nebraska) all the way to the Iowa–Missouri border in Blanchard, Iowa—which boasts a population of fewer than 50 residents—passing through certified trail towns along the way, some that are burgeoning with shops and destinations and others that are quaint and rustic.

The trail's roots go back to the Wabash Railroad—and the famous Wabash Cannonball, a passenger train that connected St. Louis and Detroit—which was one of the most important connections between the farmlands, factories, and people of the American heartland and points east in the late 19th and early 20th centuries.

The Wabash Trace Nature Trail offers many creek crossings such as this one near Imogene.

Counties
Fremont, Mills, Page, Pottawattamie

Endpoints
Iowa West Foundation Trailhead Park at E. South Omaha Bridge Road and Harry Langdon Blvd./ Valley View Trail (Council Bluffs) to N. Railroad St. just north of the Iowa–Missouri state line (Blanchard)

Mileage
62.6

Type
Rail-Trail

Roughness Index
2

Surface
Crushed Stone, Asphalt, Concrete

Wabash Trace Nature Trail

29 Valley View Trail

COUNCIL BLUFFS

80

59

6

OAKLAND

Iowa West Foundation Trailhead Park

POTTAWATTAMIE COUNTY

6

CARSON

92

START

92

Lake Manawa Trail

Wabash Avenue

Pioneer Trail

MACEDONIA

Keg Creek

500th Street

29

MINEOLA

Brothers Avenue

HENDERSON

48

SILVER CITY

287th Street

Silver Creek

Little Creek

MILLS COUNTY

59

MONTGOMERY COUNTY

34

GLENWOOD

34

HASTINGS

EMERSON

34

RED OAK

275

MALVERN

270th Street

330 Street

360 Street

STRAHAN

Walnut Creek

B Avenue

East Nishnabotna River

48

COBURG

BARTLETT

TABOR

184

IMOGENE

130th Street

H Avenue

29

275

THURMAN

370 Avenue

59

48

ESSEX

PAGE COUNTY

FREMONT COUNTY

SHENANDOAH

SIDNEY

2

FARRAGUT

2

BINGHAM

2

Missouri River

275

2

Waubonsie State Park

NEBRASKA CITY

IOWA

270th Street

COIN

P

NEBRASKA

HAMBURG

310th Street

59

NORTHBORO

FINISH

BLANCHARD

MISSOURI

N

29

0   3   6   9 miles

rails-to-trails
conservancy

Today, the Wabash Trace Nature Trail is known for its peacefulness, amazing vistas, secluded wooded sections, and encounters with wildlife. The trail also has become a social hot spot for people in the Council Bluffs and Mineola areas who enjoy Thursday night "Taco Rides," bike rides organized in the spirit of supper and good times. In Shenandoah, the annual Wabash Trace Nature Trail Marathon, Half Marathon, and Marathon Relay take place each September.

Starting in Council Bluffs, the trail begins at Iowa West Foundation Trailhead Park, where it links with the 7.2-mile Valley View Trail heading northward and the 7.5-mile Lake Manawa Trail that heads west and curves around its namesake.

Be prepared for the most populated portion of the Wabash Trace Nature Trail and the most strenuous; there are approximately 6 miles of gentle climb leaving the town heading southeast. Following the trail, you'll pass through an area known as the Loess Hills, named for the fine, wind-deposited soils that created the corrugated landscape. The Loess Hills are home to some of the best remaining native prairies and woodlands in the state and also provide crucial habitat to prairie wildlife such as red-tailed hawks.

The trail makes its way to downtown Silver City, where there are a handful of amenities, including a water fountain (one of few along the route, so a good opportunity to fill up), small stores, and a bike shop. Of note at Silver City Centennial Park—along the trail at 287th Street/Main Street and Second Street—is a time capsule that is set to be opened in 2029!

Approximately 22 miles into the route, the Malvern trailhead features water and parking, and the town offers a haven for trail users, with a pharmacy, cafés, and shops. The city square is an homage to trail users and cyclists, with interesting sculptures and murals decorating the downtown.

Your next stop is Imogene, where a unique trailhead offers restrooms and showers inside a refurbished grain bin; here, you'll also find an unpaved parking lot, picnic tables, a bike rack, and several primitive camping sites. Leaving Imogene, the trip takes on a markedly rural feel, with the crushed-stone trail giving the illusion of traveling a country road that opens up to vistas of farm fields.

Your journey will literally take you over the river and through the woods, crossing a number of waterways, including Keg Creek, Silver Creek, Little Creek, the East Nishnabotna River, Deer Creek, Hunter Branch, and countless other small streams and creeks, making this a wonderful trail for those who love scenic bridges.

History and railroad buffs will appreciate two train-car wreckages easily spotted off of the path. The first appears in Mineola, where several train cars tumble down the embankment to the left of the trail. The second is located when you cross over Silver Creek outside of Malvern; there you'll see the remnants of a 1960s train derailment with ruined boxcars lying in the riverbed.

Heading south, you'll pass through the towns of Shenandoah, Coin, and Blanchard, where the trail concludes at the Missouri border. The longest stretch between towns is less than 14 miles, so you're never too far away from civilization but are often well outside of mobile phone coverage. Trailheads at Council Bluffs, Mineola, Silver City, Imogene, and Coin offer parking, picnic tables, and bike racks.

For this rural journey, be sure to pack water, bug repellent, and a first aid kit. Trail amenities are few and far between, and you may go long stretches before encountering other trail users. It's easy to feel isolated—which for some may be a plus. What you won't generally feel is sunburned: while farmland and open sky stretch for miles on end, the original 100-foot-wide railway corridor was preserved and is often thick with trees, sometimes merging overhead to form a living canopy. For those with horses, an equestrian trail parallels the main Wabash Trace Nature Trail for 9.6 miles from Council Bluffs to Mineola.

Trail users must purchase a day pass, available at most trailheads, for $1. Annual passes are also available for $12 at the trail website.

CONTACT: wabashtrace.org

DIRECTIONS

To reach Iowa West Foundation Trailhead Park in Council Bluffs from I-29, take Exit 47 for IA 92 E, and head east for 0.7 mile. Turn right onto Harry Langdon Blvd., and go 0.7 mile. Turn right onto E. South Omaha Bridge Road, and turn right into the park. Signage for the park and the Wabash Trace Nature Trail is well marked from the street.

The closest dedicated parking to the southern endpoint is located in Shenandoah near Four Mile Creek in Waubonsie Park. To reach the parking area from IA 2, head north on A Ave., go 0.7 mile, and continue on S. Center St. for 1.3 miles. Turn right onto Ferguson Road and look for the parking lot on your right in about a half block, by Waubonsie Park. The southern endpoint is located about 17.7 miles along the trail southeast at N. Railroad St. and the Iowa–Missouri state line.

The Wapsi–Great Western Line Trail is a 19.9-mile pathway that comprises two separate segments of the former Chicago Great Western Railroad. Along the combined route, the trail passes through a plethora of backdrops, including wide, rolling landscapes, agricultural land, upland timber, wetlands, and pastures.

Elm Street to 140th Street (Elma): 5.4 miles

The southern section—also known locally as the Old Roundhouse Recreational Trail—runs for 5.4 miles from the town of Elma to its rural outskirts, passing through farmland and several tree-lined areas. The best starting point is the Elma Trailhead and Welcome Center, housed in a restored 1952 railroad depot. While the address

Counties
Howard, Mitchell

Endpoints
E. Main St. and Cherry St. (Riceville) to Walnut Ave. between 430th St. and 440th St. (Riceville) or State Line Road just east of 710th Ave. (Iowa–Minnesota state line); Elm St. and Orchard Ave. to Douglas Ave. and 140th St. (Elma)

Mileage
19.9

Type
Rail-Trail

Roughness Index
1–2

Surface
Asphalt, Crushed Stone

A picturesque railroad trestle on the Wapsi–Great Western Line Trail

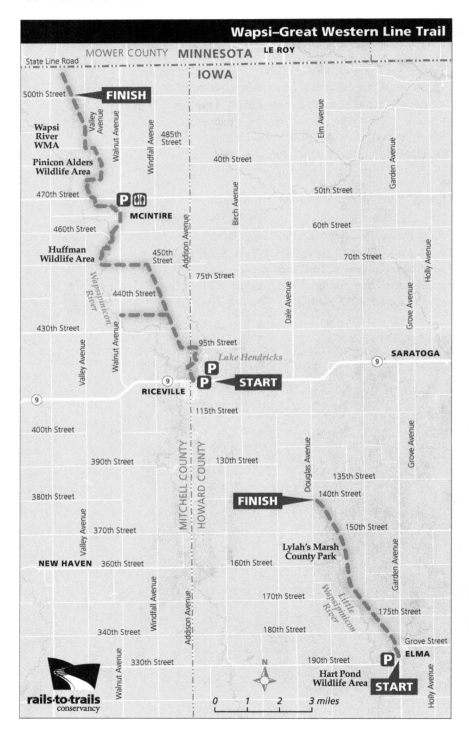

technically lists Busti Drive, you can find the parking lot for the trailhead at the corner of Elm St. and Orchard Ave.

Note Lylah's Marsh County Park about midway through your journey northward; the 32-acre open space offers a lake with boating access, shorefishing, a picnic area, trails, a playground, and restrooms.

The trail crosses Mead Creek—and the Little Wapsipinicon River multiple times—before terminating near some farm fields at Douglas Avenue and 140th Street.

CONTACT: **traveliowa.com/aspx/dest.aspx?id=9540**

DIRECTIONS

To reach the Elma Trailhead and Welcome Center from US 63, head west on 185th St., and go 5.9 miles. Continue onto IA 272/Grove St. for 1 mile, and then turn left onto Busti Ave. After 0.3 mile, turn right onto Elm St. The parking lot will be immediately to your left in front of the welcome center and an arch for the trail that says OLD ROUNDHOUSE TRAIL. There is no public parking at the northern end of this trail segment.

Riceville to the Iowa–Minnesota State Line: 14.5 miles

Beginning in suburban Riceville, the northern segment—the longer piece of pathway—travels through a variety of backdrops, including tree canopies, parklands, farm fields, and a couple small towns, before ending at the Iowa–Minnesota state line.

Heading northwest from the Riceville trailhead, you'll turn left to cross Addison Avenue and head north up Addison for a few dozen yards; note that the trail can be difficult to spot for a brief period after crossing the street. The trail picks up again and heads east and then north past Watson's Creek and the 234-acre Lake Hendricks Park, where opportunities abound for camping, fishing, boating, hiking, and more. Here, you'll also find playgrounds, picnic shelters, restrooms, and even a butterfly garden.

The trail turns left and runs parallel to 95th Street a short way before heading northwest through an agricultural area (its longest straightway) with many stream crossings and picturesque railroad trestles. At 450th Street, you'll take a sharp left to cross the Wapsipinicon River on a beautifully maintained boardwalk that traverses the surrounding wetlands. There is also an additional short segment just past 430th Street that heads west (left) to Walnut Avenue and connects to a short spur that turns north (right) to connect with 450th Street; if you take the spur, head west (left) on 450th Street to return to the main route. The path then meanders north (right) through an idyllic, well-maintained nature park filled with rolling fields of wildflowers and tall grasses; in the middle of the park, riders will find a convenient resting spot complete with bike racks and a gazebo shaded by large oak trees.

After exiting the park, you'll head northeast to McIntire; just before reaching the eastern border of town, the trail meets with First Street for a short on-road section (about a half mile). Heading north, go five blocks to Main Street (note that these blocks are on a large highway with traffic that, although minimal, is composed of very large vehicles, so use caution). Turn left onto Main Street, right onto Third Street, and then left again onto Munson Street. A sign provides instructions on how to find the off-road trail.

The off-road trail picks up again at Fourth Street on the northern border of McIntire through a tree-shaded picnic area and continues north on a concrete surface. After crossing 470th Street, you'll enter the hardwood forest of the Pinicon Alders Wildlife Area, which offers a variety of activities, including fishing, camping, and hunting. Within this area, there are several sections of the pathway that are signed as "Shared Roadway" for motorized vehicles.

The trail follows along 485th Street and Valley Avenue on the gravel roadways for just under a mile and then continues off-road on a concrete surface to the left of Valley Avenue, heading northwest. The remainder of the trail offers expansive views of farmland and a large wind farm, ending at State Line Road at the Minnesota border.

CONTACT: **wgwltrail.com**

DIRECTIONS

To reach the southern trailhead in Riceville from US 63, head west onto IA 9, and go 13 miles. Turn right into the trailhead parking lot just past Addison Ave.; the lot is by the visitor center and has a large stone Riceville sign in front.

The closest dedicated parking for the northern endpoint is in McIntire. To reach the parking area from IA 9, head north onto Walnut Ave., and go 4.7 miles. Continue on First St. for about 0.6 mile. Turn left onto Main St. in McIntire, go one block, and look for parking on your right along the block before reaching Third St.

The Waverly Rail Trail offers a pleasant, small town–meets-rural experience as it travels for 7.6 miles from downtown Waverly to its eastern endpoint north of Denver. It is also part of the Rolling Prairie Trail system, which—when complete—will travel nine communities and three counties. Beginning in Waverly at the western endpoint, you may want to take a detour about eight blocks south to explore the Bremer County Historical Society Museum, located on West Bremer Avenue and Fourth Street. Here, you'll also find a variety of small businesses, chain restaurants, and bars.

The best place to park is at the small lot on the northern end of Kohlmann Park at the intersection of Fourth Avenue Northwest and First Street Northwest. Here, you'll find picnic areas, restrooms, water fountains, and a structure that doubles as art and an amphitheater.

County
Bremer

Endpoints
Second St. NW and Sixth Ave. NW to US 63/ Larrabee Ave. south of IA 3/Denver-Jefferson Trail and Readlyn Grump Trail (Waverly)

Mileage
7.6

Type
Rail-Trail

Roughness Index
1

Surface
Asphalt, Dirt

The Waverly Trail offers a small town–meets-rural experience for trail users.

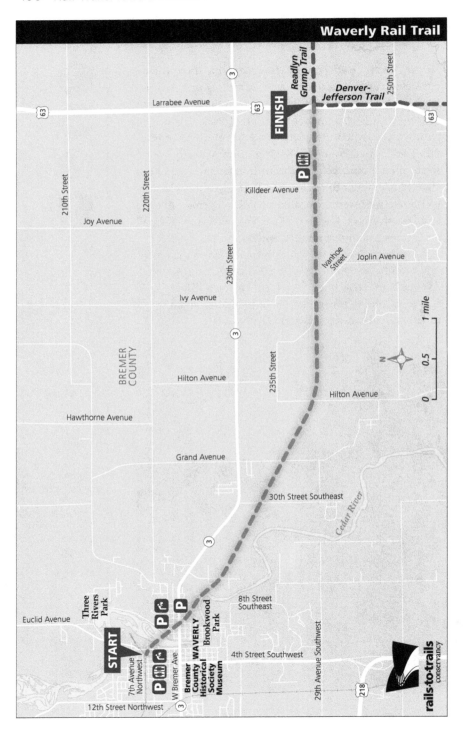

The trail begins approximately two blocks north and one block west (outside the gates of a Nestle factory) and heads southeast, crossing over the Cedar River to East Bremer Avenue—the town's main drag—and the quaint downtown area. Here, you'll find more restaurants—including a sandwich shop inside an old train station—shops, lodging, and a refurbished movie theater with an old-style neon sign displayed prominently overhead.

About a mile into your route, you'll pass several large, painted concrete planters. Leaving town, the trail becomes more wooded, with trees covering a majority of the remainder of your route and providing welcome shade in the summer months. Park benches are located throughout the trail for periodic rest stops.

The trail ends at US 63/Larrabee Avenue. From here you can continue on the Rolling Prairie Trail system by heading south on the Denver-Jefferson Trail for about 2 miles to Denver or straight on the Readlyn Grump Trail, just east of the US 63 underpass, 6 miles farther east to Readlyn.

CONTACT: **waverlyia.com/leisure-services/facilities/rail-trail-trail-system**

DIRECTIONS

Parking near the western endpoint in Waverly is available at the northern end of Kohlmann Park at Fourth Ave. NW and First St. NW (about two blocks south and one block east of the endpoint). To reach the park from US 218, take Exit 203 for IA 3 toward Waverly/Shell Rock, and head east on IA 3. Go 2.6 miles, and turn right onto W. Bremer Ave. After 1.2 miles, turn left onto First St. SW. Go about a quarter mile, and turn right onto Fourth Ave. NW. Look for parking on the right. To reach the trail's endpoint, head west on Fourth Ave. NW for one block, and then turn right onto Second St. NW. The trail begins about two blocks north, just past Sixth Ave. NW.

Another small parking area is located several blocks southeast on the northern side of Second Ave. NE between Second St. NE and Cedar Lane NE.

To reach parking near the eastern endpoint from IA 3, head south for 1 mile on Killdeer Ave. Look for a small parking area on your right just after passing the Waverly Trail. The trail endpoint is located just under 1 mile east at Larrabee Ave.

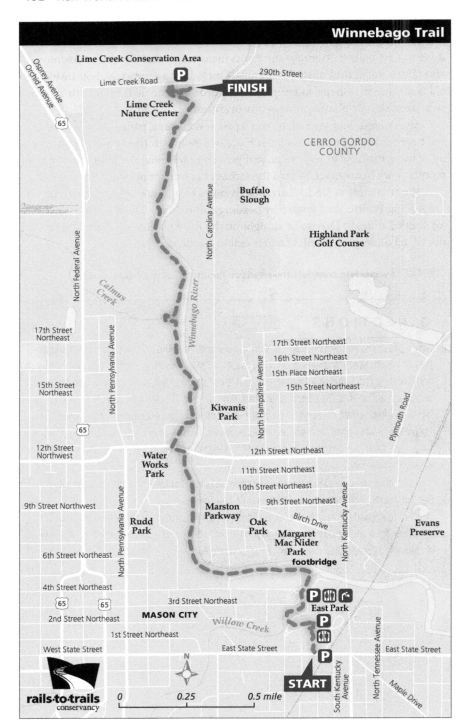

The Winnebago Trail provides the residents of Mason City with a safe, off-road link to nature, winding 3.7 miles from East Park and through residential areas to the Lime Creek Nature Center as it follows the Winnebago River. The trail is part of the River City Greenbelt & Trail System, which links the parks and cultural sites of Mason City and adjacent Clear Lake, and includes the Trolley Trail (see page 82) and the River City Trail (although the trails are not linked).

An interesting fact for Frank Lloyd Wright fans is that the small city of less than 30,000 people hosts three of the famous architect's structures: the Stockman House (First Street Northeast), designed in 1908, and the Historic Park Inn Hotel and City National Bank (West State Street)—both designed in 1909. The Historic Park Inn Hotel is the last remaining Frank Lloyd Wright hotel in the world.

Residents and visitors of the Winnebago Trail enjoy a safe, off-road link to nature in Mason City.

County
Cerro Gordo

Endpoints
East Park at E. State St. near York Ave. to Lime Creek Nature Center at the terminus of Lime Creek Road (Mason City)

Mileage
3.7

Type
Greenway/Non-Rail-Trail

Roughness Index
1

Surface
Asphalt, Gravel, Concrete

The best place to start your journey is at the East Park trailhead; here, you'll find a 1912 steam locomotive on display, a kiosk exploring the town's railroad history, ample parking, restrooms, picnic tables, a large playground, and a walk-through pergola. About a quarter mile north along the trail sits an amphitheater that hosts concerts and plays in the summer.

The trail snakes north through East Park along Willow Creek and then heads west along the Winnebago River for the remainder of its route. Just after heading west, you'll pass a short spur on your right that crosses the river and connects to the Mason City Swimming Pool.

A majority of the mostly flat route is heavily wooded, creating a serene experience for trail users. You're likely to spot a variety of small animals, birds, and butterflies, and fishing enthusiasts may wish to try their luck with the small-mouth bass and largemouth bass that inhabit the river. One word of caution: due to periodic rising waters from the Winnebago River, some low-lying sections of the trail are prone to flooding with up to a foot of water.

At the northern terminus of the trail is the Lime Creek Nature Center, established so that residents and visitors to the area could gain a better under-standing of the local environment. The center hosts various programs and events throughout the year that are open to the public.

CONTACT: traveliowa.com/aspx/trails.aspx?id=32

DIRECTIONS

To reach the southern trailhead in East Park from I-35, take Exit 190 for US 18 E/IA 27 E toward Mason City (1-mile exit). Head east on IA 27/US 18 for 6.6 miles. Take Exit 186 for US 65 toward Mason City/Downtown/Rockwell, and turn left onto US 65 N/Partridge Ave. Go 1.1 miles, and turn right onto 245th St./35th St. SE. After 1 mile, turn left onto S. Kentucky Ave./Quail Ave. Go 2.3 miles, and turn left onto E. State St. Turn right into the park, where parking is available immediately to the left and farther northwest along the park access road.

To reach the northern trailhead at Lime Creek Nature Center from I-35 N, take the exit toward 300th St., and head east out of the exit for 7.1 miles. Take a slight right onto US 65 S, and go 1.1 miles. Take a sharp left onto Nature Center Road, and go 0.5 mile. Continue right onto Lime Creek Road, and go 0.4 mile. Turn left into the parking lot. The trail is located just across the street to the right of the nature center (if you're facing the building).

The Cinder Path (see page 18) is the oldest rail-trail conversion in Iowa.

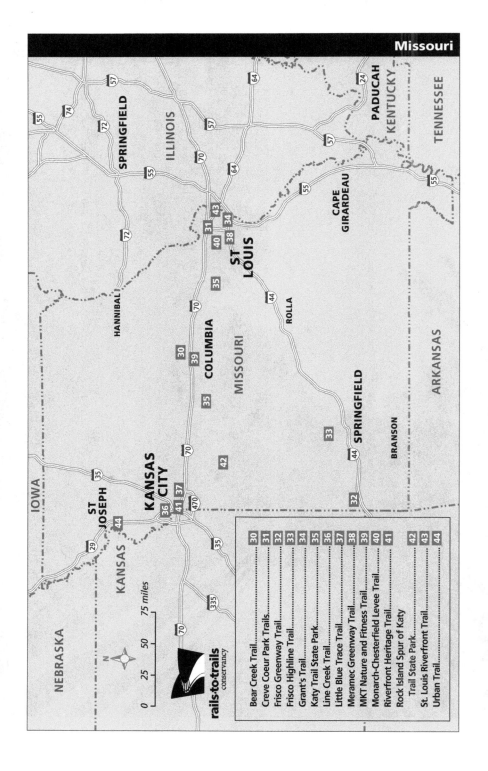

Missouri

NEBRASKA

IOWA

KANSAS

ST JOSEPH

KANSAS CITY

SPRINGFIELD

ILLINOIS

HANNIBAL

COLUMBIA

MISSOURI

ROLLA

ST LOUIS

CAPE GIRARDEAU

SPRINGFIELD

BRANSON

ARKANSAS

TENNESSEE

KENTUCKY

PADUCAH

N

0   25   50   75 miles

rails-to-trails conservancy

30 Bear Creek Trail	
31 Creve Coeur Park Trails	
32 Frisco Greenway Trail	
33 Frisco Highline Trail	
34 Grant's Trail	
35 Katy Trail State Park	
36 Line Creek Trail	
37 Little Blue Trace Trail	
38 Meramec Greenway Trail	
39 MKT Nature and Fitness Trail	
40 Monarch-Chesterfield Levee Trail	
41 Riverfront Heritage Trail	
Rock Island Spur of Katy	
42 Trail State Park	
43 St. Louis Riverfront Trail	
44 Urban Trail	

Missouri

Spanning nearly the entire state, the Katy Trail (see page 123) passes through some of Missouri's most scenic areas.

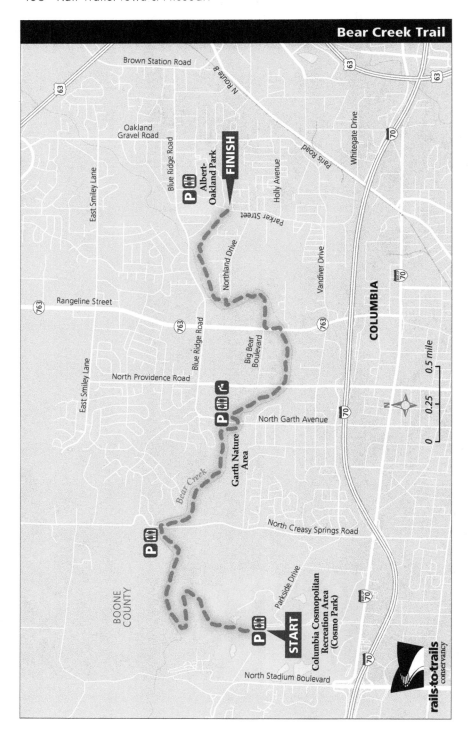

Bear Creek Trail winds across the northern half of Columbia, following Bear Creek for much of its nearly 5-mile route. Many portions of the trail traverse wooded areas, though the trail is never far from the surrounding neighborhoods. The trail has numerous access points at intersections, making it easy to ride some or all of the route, and it's well marked with signage periodically noting the mileage. Sections of the trail are washed out or feature large stones and thick, loose gravel more suited for a mountain bike, but the majority of this crushed-stone trail is hard-packed and suitable for a hybrid bike.

Starting from the trailhead at Columbia Cosmopolitan Recreation Area, commonly known as Cosmo Park, beginners should take care when riding the first 500 feet of the trail, which features a steep hill and thick gravel. Continuing on, the trail surface gradually changes to well-packed crushed stone as it passes by a quarry and through a wooded area.

The trail follows—and occasionally crosses—scenic Bear Creek.

County
Boone

Endpoints
Columbia Cosmopolitan Recreation Area to Albert-Oakland Park (Columbia)

Mileage
4.9

Type
Greenway/Non-Rail-Trail

Roughness Index
2–3

Surface
Crushed Stone, Gravel

At the 2.5-mile mark is the Garth Nature Area. To avoid a dangerous, unmarked road crossing ahead, turn right just before reaching the parking lot, restrooms, and water fountain. After taking the right, the trail loops down, passes under the road, and parallels Bear Creek.

Continuing on, the trail passes through a wooded area where tortoises, rabbits, birds, and other small wildlife are commonly seen. The trail passes under Rangeline Street and parallels the road for a short stretch. Follow the trail, which feels more like a sidewalk, as it bends to the right at Big Bear Boulevard. At the end of the road, the trail continues through woodlands.

Soon you'll cross a long, wooden bridge that overlooks Bear Creek, providing a stunning view of the creek below. The trail continues through a wooded area with plenty of fauna. Follow the signs to reach the end of the trail at Albert-Oakland Park.

CONTACT: como.gov/ParksandRec/Trails/Bear_Creek/index.php

DIRECTIONS

To reach the Columbia Cosmopolitan Recreation Area trailhead from I-70, take Exit 124 and head north onto N. Stadium Blvd. At the next light, turn right onto Bus. I-70 W. Turn left at the sign for Columbia Cosmopolitan Recreation Area and continue to go straight until you can go no farther. Turn into the adjacent parking lot and turn right again into the next parking lot, where the trail begins.

To reach the Albert-Oakland Park trailhead from US 63 N, take Exit B toward Hallsville and head south onto N. Route B. Turn right onto Brown Station Road and left onto Blue Ridge Road. A little less than a mile down the road, turn left into the park entrance.

The Creve Coeur Park Trails are a collection of paved pathways winding through wetland and wooded areas within St. Louis County's first and largest park, which spans more than 2,000 acres. (When the west end of the trail crosses the Missouri River, it enters St. Charles County.)

The trail's Lakeview Loop offers a 3.7-mile trip around the sizable Creve Coeur Lake, replete with well-used picnic shelters and opportunities to access the water from several points. Throughout the summer, you can experience the lake by kayak, available for rent. On the west side of the lake, the 2.8-mile Meadows Loop circles the Gateway Sports Athletic Field Complex. Restrooms and water fountains are available in this area, and several hiking-only trails can be found on the east side of the lake, offering a diverse outdoor recreation experience.

The trail winds through wooded areas within St. Louis County's largest park.

Counties
St. Louis, St. Charles

Endpoints
Creve Coeur Lake Memorial Park (St. Louis) to Katy Trail at Page Ave./ MO 364 (St. Charles)

Mileage
11.5

Type
Greenway/Non-Rail-Trail

Roughness Index
1

Surface
Asphalt

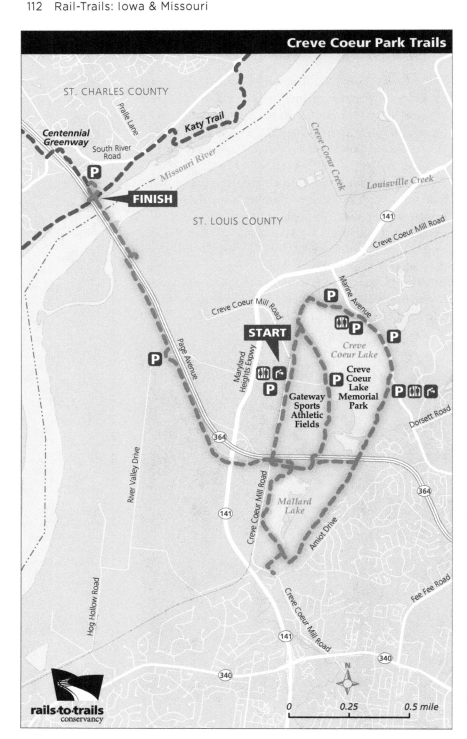

Creve Coeur Park Trails

ST. CHARLES COUNTY

Pralie Lane

Centennial
Greenway

Katy Trail

South River
Road

Creve Coeur Creek

Missouri River

Louisville Creek

FINISH

ST. LOUIS COUNTY

141

Creve Coeur Mill Road

Creve Coeur Mill Road

Marine Avenue

START

Creve
Coeur Lake

Page Avenue

Maryland
Heights Expwy

Creve
Coeur
Lake
Memorial
Park

Gateway
Sports
Athletic
Fields

364

Dorsett Road

364

River Valley Drive

141

Creve Coeur Mill Road

Mallard
Lake

Amiot Drive

Hog Hollow Road

Creve Coeur Mill Road

141

Fee Fee Road

340

340

N

rails·to·trails
conservancy

0   0.25   0.5 mile

At the southern end of the park, the trail system loops around the smaller Mallard Lake, where you're likely to see herons, egrets, and other waterfowl.

Between the two lakes is Page Avenue (MO 364), which bisects the park. If you pick up the trail that parallels the roadway and heads west out of the park, you'll be on the 2.8-mile Creve Coeur Connector segment of the trail system. At the outset, you'll pedal up a short, fairly steep hill, but then the trail will level out and you'll soon cross a bridge spanning the Missouri River. On the other side, you can connect to the Katy Trail (see page 123), which follows the river and spans nearly 240 miles across the state.

Although the Creve Coeur Connector parallels the highway, the landscape to the west is beautiful with native prairie grasses, a marsh, and wildflowers in the spring. As with most of this collection of trails, birds of all types can be enjoyed as you continue along this easily traversed section.

About a quarter mile from the Katy Trail intersection, you can also connect to the Centennial Greenway. This short section of that trail leads up to the St. Charles County Heritage Museum; ultimately, the developing Centennial Greenway will stretch 20 miles.

CONTACT: **stlouisco.com/parksandrecreation/trails/crevecoeurtrails**

DIRECTIONS

To reach Creve Coeur Lake Memorial Park, take I-270 to the Page Ave./MO 364 exit, heading west. On Page Avenue, take the second exit (Exit 17) to the Maryland Heights Expy. and turn right to go north. At the second stoplight, turn right (east) onto Creve Coeur Mill Road. After the railroad crossing, the Creve Coeur Lake Memorial Park entrance will appear on the left. Several parking lots are available in the park.

To get to the parking lot just before the Katy Trail from MO 364, take Exit 14 and turn right (east) onto Arena Pkwy. After 0.4 mile, turn right onto South River Road, and then left into the parking lot.

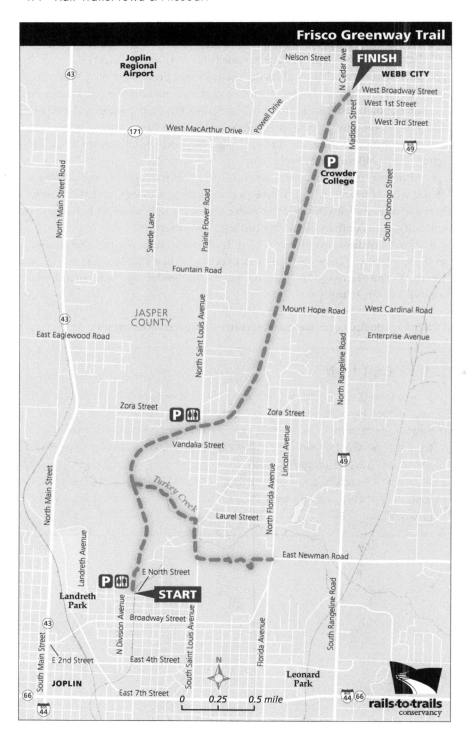

Frisco Greenway Trail

The southern terminus of the Frisco Greenway Trail is tucked into an unassuming neighborhood in Joplin. From there, the gravel trail winds 4.2 miles northward along the former St. Louis–San Francisco Railway, from whence it gets its name. At the trailhead, users will find a gravel parking lot and portable toilet. There is no drinkable water along the trail or at either trail end, so make sure to bring a filled bottle with you. Before beginning the journey, it may be worth a short side trip over to Landreth Park, which lies five blocks west of the southern end of the trail; in the park, you'll find drinking water, restrooms, picnic tables, and other amenities.

After 0.8 mile, you can turn right onto a paved spur that runs along Turkey Creek for a 1.4-mile stretch through rural neighborhoods and farms.

The greenway is covered in lush foliage, and, on most days, you will pass local residents enjoying the cool,

Near the southern end of the trail, you'll cross scenic Turkey Creek.

County
Jasper

Endpoints
E. North St. and
N. Division Ave. (Joplin)
to N. Cedar Ave. and
W. Broadway St.
(Webb City)

Mileage
5.6

Type
Rail-Trail

Roughness Index
1–2

Surface
Asphalt, Gravel

shaded corridor for strolls and jogs. As you make the trip from Joplin to Webb City, you will cross several small roads. A couple of these crossings are marked with wooden trail signage, which ensures that passing drivers take note and slow down for trail users. Traffic is light in this area, but make sure to stop and check that no cars are coming before crossing roads.

The trail's northern terminus in Webb City does not have restroom or water facilities and is not marked with signage. However, it does have an easily accessible, off-road gravel area for you to pull a vehicle into and load up or off.

You will notice that both communities of Webb City and Joplin are experiencing a good bit of commercial and residential growth around the trail, and there are plans to extend the Frisco Greenway Trail from either end.

CONTACT: **joplin-trails-coalition.webnode.com/frisco-greenway-trail**

DIRECTIONS

To reach the Joplin trailhead from Bus. I-44/MO 66/E. 7th St. westbound, turn right onto S. Main St., heading north for five blocks. Turn right onto Second St., which soon becomes E. Broadway St. Take E. Broadway St. for 0.5 mile and take a left onto N. Division Ave. Travel four blocks and then take a right onto E. North St. Take your first left into the parking lot for the Frisco Greenway trailhead.

To reach the Webb City trailhead from Bus. I-49/E. MacArthur Drive/MO 171 westbound, take a right onto S. Madison St. Travel north for five blocks and turn left onto W. Broadway St. Before the end of the block (just before reaching S. Cedar Avenue), you will see the gravel pull-off area and the beginning of the trail on your left.

The 37.6-mile, partially paved Frisco Highline Trail connects Bolivar and Springfield with plenty to see along the way. If you travel from north to south, you'll find that the corridor rises at about a 3% grade, so you'll have a bit of a workout. If you prefer to ride downhill, take the trip in reverse by starting at the Springfield end.

Parking can be found at both terminuses of the trail. The northern terminus, located just past an art-covered bridge, provides access to bathroom facilities and a water fountain. Be sure to fill up with plenty of water as additional fountains are sparse until about mile 20.

From Bolivar, the first 4 miles are nicely paved and maintained. However, about 2 miles into the trip, trail users will need to take a short on-road detour around busy MO 13, which will add a couple of miles to your adventure but make for a much safer journey to the rest of the trail.

The northern and southern ends of the Frisco Highline Trail are nicely paved.

Counties
Greene, Polk

Endpoints
N. Claud Ave. and W. Fair
Play St. (Bolivar) to
W. Kearney St. and N.
Rural Ave. (Springfield)

Mileage
37.6

Type
Rail-Trail

Roughness Index
1–2

Surface
Asphalt, Gravel

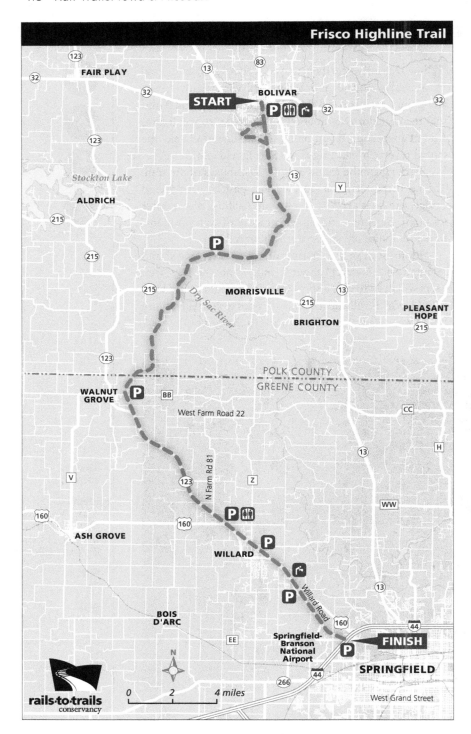

Brave locals look for a break in traffic and hurry across this road, but this is not recommended. See detour directions below.

The paved portion of the trail picks back up on the other side of MO 13 and, for the next 3 miles, you will travel through rural farmland and see cows and horses grazing and lounging in the shade on the nearby farms. The landscape is dotted with hundreds of wildflowers and inhabited by a variety of birds, chipmunks, and rabbits.

After mile 4, and for the next 22 miles to Willard, the trail is not paved and the surface is much rougher with medium-size gravel and sporadic potholes. Keep an eye out for the cattle guards that run along the path as well; they could be a hazard if you step into them or accidentally get a bike tire caught between the bars. On the bright side, this segment of the Frisco Highline Trail has very nice, shady tree cover, and is dotted with many small bridges that run over babbling creeks and larger streams. At mile 20, you will arrive at the Walnut Grove trailhead. You'll find a gravel parking lot here, and it's a good spot to take a break, have lunch, or exit the trail.

Continue on from Walnut Grove for 8 miles toward the town of Willard. At Willard, the trail becomes paved and the surrounding area is much more commercialized and dotted with trailside convenience stores, ice-cream shops, and bike depots that provide free water and air for tires. This last stretch of the trail runs through a suburban landscape, and you'll be pedaling past homes and schools. The trail ends in a paved parking lot near a hotel and commercial district in Springfield.

CONTACT: friscohighlinetrail.org

DIRECTIONS

To reach the Bolivar trailhead, from the intersection of MO 13 and W. Broadway St., turn onto W. Broadway St. toward the center of town, and follow it for 1.6 miles. Take a left onto W. Fair Play St. and follow signs to the Frisco Highline Trail. The trailhead is just past an art-covered bridge.

To reach the Springfield trailhead, from the intersection of US 160 and I-44, heading away from town, follow US 160 south for 0.2 mile to W. Kearney St. and turn right. Stay on W. Kearney St. for 0.2 mile, and the trailhead parking lot will be on your right.

To take the on-road detour about 2 miles from the north terminus in Bolivar, take a right onto W. Aldrich Road. Follow this road for about a mile and take a left onto S. 107th Road and then take the first left onto Prairie Lane. In a half mile, Prairie Lane meets back up with the trail.

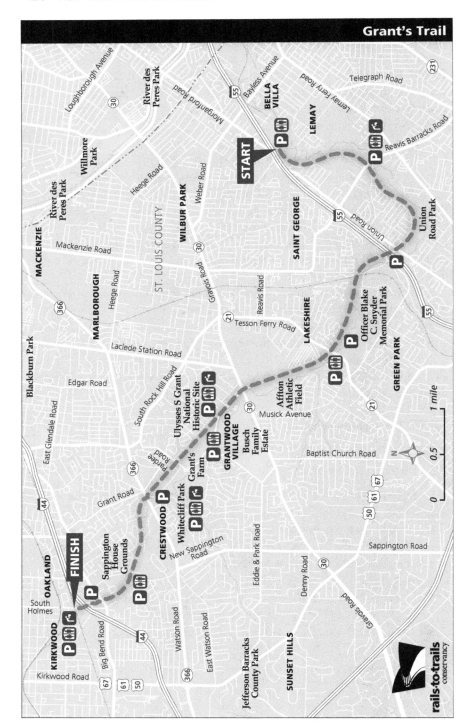

Honoring former President Ulysses S. Grant, this flat and relaxed 7.9-mile trail is easily accessible from downtown St. Louis. Grant's Trail is well maintained with plentiful restrooms and drinking water facilities along the way. The route accommodates both functional and recreational uses while facilitating a historically and visually engaging experience. While the trail does require the user to navigate many street crossings, they are well signaled to promote safety, including a four-way stop that gives bicyclists the same status as cars!

You'll find access to several historical sites along the trail, including Grant's Farm, home to the 1850s four-room log cabin that the famed general and president built, as well as White Haven, another home owned by Grant and now operated by the National Park Service. While at White Haven, Grant approved construction of the Pacific Railroad

County
St. Louis

Endpoints
Orlando Gardens
near Hoffmeister Ave.
(Lemay) to Leffingwell
Ave. at Holmes Ave.
(Kirkwood)

Mileage
7.9

Type
Rail-Trail

Roughness Index
1

Surface
Asphalt

On the trail's eastern end, you'll find wooded areas and creek crossings.

(later known as the Missouri Pacific Railroad) through his property. Ground was broken for the railway in 1851, and it was billed at the time as "The First Railroad West of the Mississippi." Grant's Trail is built on the former Kirkwood-Carondelet Branch of the rail line.

Starting from Orlando Gardens on the trail's east end, wooded areas complemented by creek crossings create a delightful experience. After 1.3 miles, you'll arrive at the former Trailnet office that sits trailside at 3900 Reavis Barracks Road. This community development organization, which took the lead in collaborating with local and state government entities to create the trail, invites you to stop at their trailside outdoor seating area, where you'll also find restrooms and drinking water.

Just over 4 miles later, Grant's Farm, featuring an animal park and the Anheuser-Busch Clydesdale pastures, will come up on your left. Just beyond Grant's Farm, consider stopping at Whitecliff Park with its wooded trails and other recreational facilities. To get there, turn left when the trail intersects Pardee Road; after only a tenth of a mile on this residential road, you'll see the entrance sign for the park.

Two miles farther down the trail, you'll cross I-44 on a bike-pedestrian bridge. If you're up for more riding, you can continue pedaling on-road into downtown Kirkwood. From the trailhead, head north on South Holmes Avenue for 0.6 mile and turn left onto East Argonne Drive. In 0.8 mile, you'll arrive at Kirkwood Station, a renovated 1893 depot, which is still in use today as an Amtrak train station.

Plans to extend the trail farther are continuing. Grant's Trail is part of the larger Gravois Creek Greenway and plays an increasingly key link in the River Ring, a growing 600-mile network of interconnected trails and on-street bicycle routes throughout the St. Louis region.

CONTACT: stlouisco.com/parksandrecreation/trails/grantstrail or bikegrantstrail.com

DIRECTIONS

To reach the Orlando Gardens trailhead from St. Louis, take I-55 south and exit at Union Road; then turn left onto Hoffmeister Ave. After a short distance, you will see the large parking lot on your right.

To reach the Kirkwood trailhead from St. Louis, take I-44 to Exit 279 for Berry Road; keep left at the fork to continue toward S. Berry Road. Turn left onto S. Berry Road, then right onto Big Bend Blvd. After 0.6 mile, turn right onto Melshire Ave. and, after 0.2 mile, take a right onto Holmes Ave. Very shortly thereafter, the trailhead parking lot will appear on your left.

A t nearly 240 miles long, Katy Trail State Park spans nearly the full width of Missouri and is the country's longest continuous rail-trail, intersecting with rural farmland, scenic small towns, and centers of commerce and government on its route paralleling the Missouri River. Along the way, it invites its walkers, runners, and riders on a journey to explore the history of the state.

On the east side of Missouri, the trail officially begins in Machens at mile marker 26.9 (the Katy Trail follows the old railroad mileage system, based on the former rail line's genesis in St. Louis). To access this endpoint, trail users can park at the Black Walnut trailhead at mile marker 29 and bike or walk in past adjacent agricultural fields. Many users choose instead to jump on at mile marker 39.5 in the historic town of St. Charles, where the trail threads between the state's first capitol building and a restored

Trail's End Monument celebrates Sedalia's history as a cow town after the Civil War.

Counties
Boone, Callaway, Cole, Cooper, Henry, Howard, Montgomery, Pettis, St. Charles, Warren

Endpoints
Machens Road near MO 94 (Machens) to E. Sedalia Ave. near Price Lane (Clinton)

Mileage
239.6

Type
Rail-Trail

Roughness Index
2

Surface
Crushed Stone, Gravel

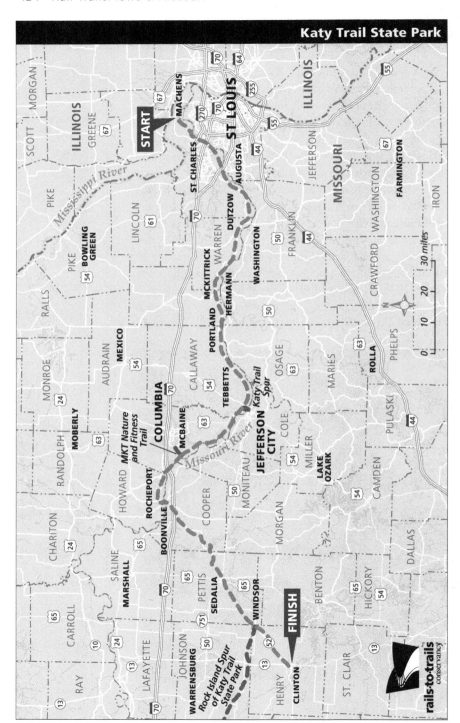

Katy Trail State Park

depot building. Trail riders can take advantage of trailside businesses here, including a bike shop, café, brewery, and several historical B&Bs.

The trail continues along the riverbank to mile marker 66.3 in Augusta, which features a brewery and a bike shop right next to the trail, as well as several scenic wineries and B&Bs just up the hill. It continues on through fertile floodplains to Dutzow (mile marker 74) and McKittrick (mile marker 100.8), both of which provide jumping-off points to catch the Amtrak Missouri River Runner train across the river in Washington and Hermann, respectively. With advance reservations, cyclists can bring their bikes aboard for a $10 fee. Equestrians can ride horses on this stretch between Portland (mile marker 115.9) and Tebbetts (mile marker 131.2).

At North Jefferson (mile marker 143.2), riders can take the Katy Trail Spur into Jefferson City, Missouri's capital, via a three-story bicycle ramp and a protected bike lane on the bridge over the Missouri River. From here, open fields alongside the trail give way to trees shading the path and scenic bridges transporting riders across numerous waterways. Just west of McBaine (mile marker 169.5), riders can branch off toward Columbia on the MKT Nature and Fitness Trail (see page 137), a popular 9.3-mile urban getaway featuring a mountain bike skills course near its midpoint.

As the Katy Trail carries on toward Rocheport (mile marker 178.3), trail users pass towering bluffs carved by the Missouri River and approach the trail's only tunnel, cut through solid rock. During their famous Corps of Discovery expedition, Meriwether Lewis and William Clark wrote about "curious paintings" left by Native Americans on the projection of limestone here.

In Boonville (mile marker 191.8), riders may wish to check on the restoration progress of the original MKT rail bridge. Although Katy Trail traffic currently routes over the adjacent US 40 bridge, the preservation of the original MKT rail bridge serves a critical role in keeping the Katy Trail's railbanked corridor legally intact. At this point, the trail crosses and deviates from the Missouri River to head southwest toward Sedalia (mile marker 229), home to a fully restored trailside depot that offers a wide range of Katy Trail memorabilia for sale.

At Windsor (mile marker 248), trail users will want to check out the new Rock Island Spur of Katy Trail State Park (see page 147), which stretches nearly 50 miles to Pleasant Hill, a suburb of Kansas City. Eventually, more rail-trail will be developed through the Rock Island corridor heading east to connect with the Katy a second time near Washington.

Equestrians can ride between Sedalia and Clinton (mile marker 264.6), the western terminus of the Katy Trail, as well as a section in the middle between Portland and Tebbetts.

CONTACT: **mostateparks.com/park/katy-trail-state-park**

Former railroad bridges and other historical treasures dot the rail-trail.

DIRECTIONS

To reach the eastern trailhead from I-70, take Exit 228 onto MO 94/First Capitol Drive. Turn northwest onto MO 94 (toward downtown St. Charles) and follow signs for MO 94 for 7.2 miles. At intersection with MO H, continue straight on MO H for an additional 4.8 miles. At the intersection with Music Ferry Road, turn right onto Music Ferry Road. The Black Walnut trailhead and parking lot will be on your right in 0.1 mile at the intersection of Music Ferry Road and Black Walnut Road. The Machens trailhead is inaccessible by car, but trail users can reach it by traveling along the Katy Trail by bike or foot 2.1 miles northeast of the Black Walnut trailhead (across the street and heading away from Black Walnut Road).

To reach the Clinton trailhead from I-49, take Exit 141 onto MO 18 E. Follow MO 18 E for 31.2 miles, and then turn left onto NW 401 Road. Follow NW 401 Road for 1 mile, and turn right to stay on NW 401 Road for an additional 0.1 mile before it intersects with MO 7 S. Follow MO 7 S for 3.8 miles; then take the exit for MO 52 W for 0.2 mile. At the intersection with Price Lane, turn left; then take an immediate right into the parking lot. The Clinton trailhead will be on your right.

The Line Creek Trail is about all you can ask for as a trail lover. This beautifully paved 8-mile trail winds serenely through Platte County and has a little bit of everything for everyone. Traveling north from the southern terminus in Riverside near the Missouri–Kansas border, you will wind through neighborhoods and heavily wooded areas. There are several scenic spots along Line Creek to take a photo, including a beautiful, small waterfall along the creek bank about a mile and a half into the trip.

The trail is quite hilly, so, while short, the Line Creek Trail is challenging for someone looking to get a good walking, riding, or running workout. Many of the nearby residents can be found doing just that; on a beautiful Missouri day, you will see many adults, kids, and pets enjoying the shady Line Creek corridor and its on-trail amenities. The trail offers mile markers along its entire length, and

The trail is quite hilly, offering a good workout.

County
Platte

Endpoints
Argosy Pkwy. and Argosy Casino Pkwy. (Riverside) to N. Line Creek Pkwy. and NW Old Stagecoach Road (Kansas City)

Mileage
8.4

Type
Rail-Trail

Roughness Index
1

Surface
Concrete

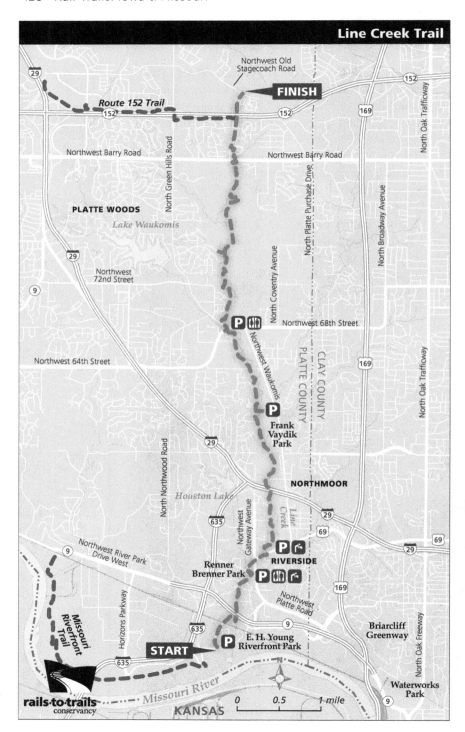

there are several easily accessible trailheads with parking and bathroom facilities at various points along the trail.

As you near the end of the trail, it intersects with North Line Creek Parkway, a neighborhood street. Cross the parkway's large median and take a right to continue along the last 0.8 mile of the trail; note that the trail's character will change here and it will look like a wide sidewalk. After about a half mile, the Line Creek Trail intersects the nicely paved Route 152 Trail. Stay straight another 0.3 mile to follow the trail and cross over MO 152 to reach the end of the Line Creek Trail in Kansas City.

CONTACT: platteparks.com/line-creek-trail

DIRECTIONS

To reach the Riverside trailhead at the southern end of the trail from I-635 northbound, take Exit 9 for Argosy Casino Pkwy. Take a left onto Horizons Pkwy. and follow the traffic circle around to the Argosy Casino Pkwy. exit. From the traffic circle, take Argosy Casino Pkwy. east for 1.2 miles to the trail parking lot.

Little Blue Trace Trail

East Union School Road

FINISH

East Union School Road   East Yocum Road

East Blue Mills Road

291

P

24

7

East Kentucky Road

Whitney Road

24

Little Blue Parkway

North Ferguson Spring Road

North Powell Road

INDEPENDENCE

P

East Bundschu Road

North Twyman Road

24

East Salisbury Road

South Jones Road

South Powell Road

P   78

291

78

7

East Truman Road

Burr Oak Woods Conservation Area

Holke Road

78

Holke Road

South Little Blue Parkway

P

East R D Mize Road

Little Blue River

East Eureka Road

East Pink Hill Road

Burr Oak Woods Conservation Area and Nature Center

East 39th Street South

291

P

Hartman Heritage Center

East 39th Street South

70

Lees Summit Road

Lee's Summit Road

40

KANSAS CITY

70

LAKE TAPAWINGO

START

470

Blue Springs Lake

40

N

Little Blue Trace County Park

0   1   2 miles

rails·to·trails
conservancy

Located outside of bustling Kansas City, this beautiful, partially paved, 15-mile riverside pathway is a favorite for locals and visitors alike. Unlike many of the rural trails that you find in Missouri, the Little Blue Trace Trail runs through several busy suburbs of Kansas City, causing the corridor itself to be relatively populated at all times of day.

The southern trailhead is not marked with signage and there is no parking, just a place to pull off the road and enter through a gate. However, 3.7 miles north of the trail's southern terminus, you'll find parking in a bustling shopping and dining area called Hartman Heritage Center, located off S. Little Blue Parkway just north of I-70.

The trail has excellent picnic and bathroom amenities all along the way, and there are several strategically placed emergency call buttons should trail users find themselves needing help.

County
Jackson

Endpoints
Phelps Road at NW Lee's Summit Road (Kansas City) to E. Old Blue Mills Road just south of E. Blue Mills Road (Independence)

Mileage
15.1

Type
Greenway/Non-Rail-Trail

Roughness Index
1–2

Surface
Asphalt, Crushed Stone

The trail winds along the Little Blue River for its entire length.

Lined with yellow wildflowers in the summer, the trail passes under several old train trestles and more modern overpasses. At mile marker 7, be sure to stop for a picture at a small waterfall. Here you may even catch a glimpse of a pair of resident snapping turtles. Also of note, several well-marked parking accesses dot the second half of the trail, making it very easy to begin your trip at a variety of points along the way.

Take caution because a couple of times on the trail you will have to make a steep climb up to a main road where you take a brief off-road paved path to return to the trail via a fairly steep drop-off with turns. The trail is plenty wide and nicely paved and maintained in each of these instances, but it is still important to be careful of your speed. The trail ends in a nice park with parking.

CONTACT: makeyourdayhere.com/Facilities/Facility/Details/Little-Blue-Trace-12

DIRECTIONS

The closest parking lot to the southern end of the trail is in Hartman Heritage Center, a shopping and dining area. From I-70, take Exit 17 for Little Blue Pkwy. Head north on the parkway; shortly thereafter, you will come to E. Jackson Drive. Take a left onto E. Jackson Drive to enter the commercial area. On E. Jackson Drive, take your first right turn into a parking lot; toward the back of this lot, you'll see a playground, portable toilet, and the trail access point. To reach the southern trailhead, travel 3.7 miles southwest along the trail to Phelps Road at NW Lee's Summit Road.

To reach the northern trailhead from Independence, travel eastbound on US 24 until you see the exit for N. Twyman Road. Take a left and stay on N. Twyman Road for 1.1 miles. Turn left onto E. Blue Mills Road and continue on the roadway for 0.9 mile. Take a left onto E. Old Blue Mills Road and the trailhead will appear immediately on your left.

The Meramec Greenway Trail is planned to one day encompass 50 miles throughout the St. Louis metro region, expanding as far west as Pacific, Missouri. The scenic route connects residents to the Meramec River and many parks in the region as it winds along the river and limestone bluffs, and through woodlands and the heart of several communities. Just over 20 miles of the greenway are open in the five disconnected segments outlined below from west to east.

In Eureka, the trail begins at Lions Park, which offers parking, restrooms, and picnic pavilions. From there, the paved trail heads west for 2.7 miles, ending at the much larger Route 66 State Park. Over an expanse of more than 400 acres, the park offers hiking, biking, and horseback-riding trails, as well as river access for boating and fishing.

North of Eureka, another segment of the trail begins in the small community of Glencoe and spans nearly 6 miles; you'll find a trailhead with parking at the end of

As much of the trail is heavily wooded, you're likely to see white-tailed deer and other wildlife.

County
St. Louis

Endpoints
Lions Park (Eureka) to Lower Meramec Park (St. Louis)

Mileage
20.2

Type
Rail-Trail

Roughness Index
1–2

Surface
Asphalt, Crushed Stone

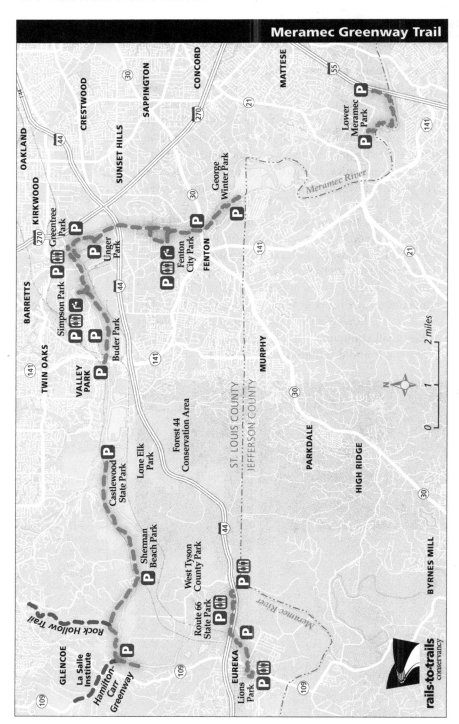

Meramec Greenway Trail

Grand Avenue. This section of the greenway, known as the Al Foster Memorial Trail, has a crushed-stone surface and is heavily wooded. As you travel east along the river from the trailhead, you'll follow the route of the former Missouri Pacific Railroad and enjoy the sight of soaring limestone cliffs and perhaps wildlife, especially white-tailed deer. If you head north from the trailhead (away from the river), you will be on the Hamilton-Carr Greenway, which takes travelers past the La Salle Institute campus and toward the Rockwoods Reservation. Farther along, you'll also have the opportunity to connect to the Rock Hollow Trail. From there, the Al Foster Memorial Trail heads southeast, crossing under an active railroad trestle and entering Sherman Beach Park, where there's another trailhead with parking. The trail continues east to its end in Castlewood State Park.

After a gap, the trail picks up again in the city of Valley Park. This segment is paved and stretches 3.5 miles from the Arnold's Grove trailhead to Greentree Park in Kirkwood along the north bank of the river. Wonderful river views, a public boat launch, and distinct orange-hued sand make it a memorable experience. For the young at heart, Greentree Park also offers a remote-controlled car track. Midway, you can cross Marshall Road to enter Simpson Park, which encompasses forested areas and a large lake. You'll also find restrooms and water here.

On the other side of the river, 6 more miles of paved trail roll out from Unger Memorial County Park, where herons, egrets, and other waterfowl can frequently be found in the park's shallow lake. South of the park, you'll pass a major soccer park and then a baseball complex before traveling under the interstate and into the town of Fenton. A short section of the route is on-road along Riverside Drive before becoming trail again in Fenton City Park, where you can stop for restrooms and water. The trail ends at George Winter Park on the banks of the Meramec River.

The last open segment is a paved, 2-mile section completely within the county's Lower Meramec Park. Thick river lowland forest dominates this trail. Waterfowl and other wildlife are plentiful here. Trailheads with parking are available at either end of the segment.

CONTACT: **greatriversgreenway.org/meramec-greenway-master-plan**

DIRECTIONS

To reach the western end of the trail in Eureka's Lions Park from I-44 eastbound, take Exit 264 for MO 109 S. After traveling 0.8 mile on MO 109, turn right onto Legends Pkwy. After 0.1 mile, turn right onto Bald Hill Road. Travel north on the roadway for 0.3 mile to the parking lot in the park, which will be on your right.

To reach the Al Foster Memorial Trail from I-44/US 50 in Eureka, take Exit 264 for MO 109 N. Follow MO 109 for 2.9 miles, then turn right onto Old State Road. Take the next right onto Washington Ave., which becomes Grand Ave.; stay on the roadway, traveling 0.4 mile to the trailhead parking lot, which will be on your left.

To reach the Arnold's Grove trailhead from I-44, take Exit 272 and merge onto MO 141 N. Travel 1 mile, just past the bridge over the Meramec River, and turn left onto Marshall Road. Take an immediate left turn onto Meramec Station Road, heading south. The trailhead is at the end of the road.

To reach the George Winter Park trailhead in Fenton from I-270, take Exit 3 for MO 30/ Gravois Road. Turn left onto Gravois Road and then take an immediate left turn onto Weber Hill Road, followed by a quick right turn onto Gravois Road. Travel 2.2 miles west and cross the river into Fenton. Take a left onto S. Old Highway 141 and follow it south for 0.6 mile. Turn left onto Allen Road and go 0.5 mile. Turn left (east) toward the river, followed by a hard left turn onto Deer Lodge Road. The trailhead is at a dead end just ahead.

To reach the trail in Lower Meramec Park from I-55, take Exit 193 for Meramec Bottom Road. Turn right onto Meramec Bottom Road, then take your next left onto Krumm Road, which will dead-end at the park's parking lot.

The MKT Nature and Fitness Trail spans just over 9 miles between the famed Katy Trail State Park (see page 123), which stretches across Missouri, and Columbia. It gets its name from the former spur line of the Missouri-Kansas-Texas (MKT) Railroad, which it follows.

Its southern trailhead in McBaine offers a paved parking lot, bathrooms, and drinking water. Carefully follow the signage marking the start of the trail. After crossing Perche Creek, stay to the right at the trail fork to follow the MKT Trail; the Katy Trail continues to the left of the fork.

The first half of the MKT is rural and cuts through wooded areas and sprawling farmland while following nearby Perche and Hinkson Creeks. The crushed stone along this portion of the trail is well packed and easily passable by hybrid bike. Road bikes may also be suited to this terrain. Enjoy the sights, sounds, and flora and fauna

County
Boone

Endpoints
Katy Trail State Park at MO K (McBaine) to Flat Branch Park at S. Fourth St. and Cherry St. (Columbia)

Mileage
9.3

Type
Rail-Trail

Roughness Index
1

Surface
Concrete, Crushed Stone

The MKT Nature and Fitness Trail offers shady tree cover during the summer.

MKT Nature and Fitness Trail

COLUMBIA

FINISH

East Broadway

Peace Park

University of Missouri

(763)

(740)

Flat Branch Park

(163)

Grindstone Nature Area

Hinkson Creek Trail

South Providence Road

(163)

(163)

West Nifong Boulevard

Cosmo-Bethel Park

Southampton Drive

Cedar Lake

West Boulevard South

(740)

Flat Branch

Kiwanis Park

County House Trail

West Broadway

(740)

South Fairview Road

Rock Bridge Memorial State Park

West Vawter School Road

South Sinclair Road

Bonnie View Nature Sanctuary

Hinkson Woods Conservation Area

Scott Boulevard

South Scott Boulevard

1 mile

0.5

N

0

South Brushwood Lake Road

South Howard Orchard Road

Perche Creek

MCBAINE

K

START

Katy Trail State Park

UU

rails-to-trails
conservancy

of the Missouri countryside as you pass through a patchwork of shaded and exposed corridor. The second half of the trail is fully canopied, and you cross over several old wooden bridges across Flat Branch Creek.

The trail is dotted with bathroom, parking, and water facilities along its entire length and has some of the best amenities of any trail in the state. The closer you get toward the center of Columbia, the more populated you will find the trail. Runners, walkers, bikers, and students from the local University of Missouri campus fill the trail, especially along the last 3 miles.

The trail splits in the last 0.5 mile as you enter town, but stay to the left to pass through a small tunnel and travel by a lovely water feature and into Flat Branch Park, where you'll find a picnic area, drinking water, and parking. From here, you're only a short way from Columbia's charming downtown.

CONTACT: **como.gov/ParksandRec/Parks/MKT_Trail**

DIRECTIONS

To reach the southern trailhead from Columbia, take MO 163/Providence Road south to a right onto E. Nifong Blvd. Continue on the roadway westbound as it becomes W. Vawter School Road. You could take a right onto Scott Blvd. to a trail access point and parking, or continue straight on what is now S. Brushwood Lake Road. Continuing on this roadway as it heads south and becomes S. Howard Orchard Road will bring you to a T-intersection with MO KK; take a right onto MO KK, and then another immediate right onto MO K. As you pass the Columbia Water Plant, look for the sign directing you into the trailhead parking lot.

To reach the northern trailhead in Columbia from I-70, take Exit 126. Take a left onto MO 163/N. Providence Road. Travel south until you reach Locust St. and take a left. Take your next left onto S. Fourth St. You'll see parking spots on either side of the street.

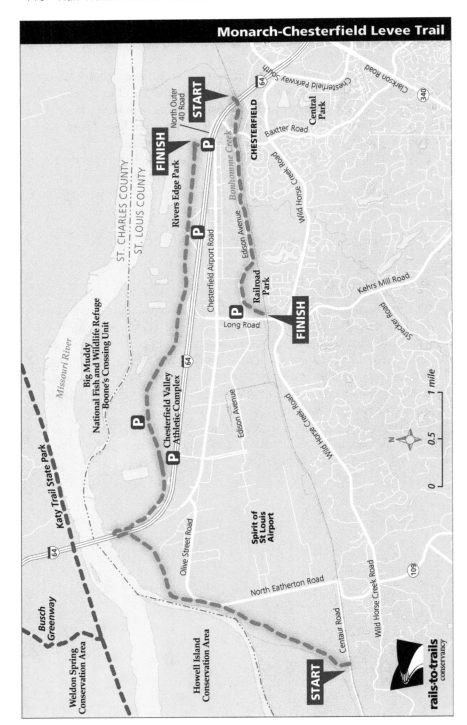

Monarch-Chesterfield Levee Trail

The Greater St. Louis area is dominated by the "Great Rivers." While the Mississippi River gets most of the attention, the Missouri River is not one to be taken for granted. An emerging trail system along the Missouri is forming, which offers more than 10 miles of paved trail in two disconnected sections. The Monarch-Chesterfield Levee Trail provides an interesting way to see the river and to get around the developing suburb of Chesterfield.

Beginning at Centaur Road on the western end of the longer segment, you are immediately high above the surrounding landscape on top of the levee. A wonderfully maintained asphalt surface is a constant enjoyment along this trail. Sights include farm fields and heavy timber at the river's edge, as well as some great airplane viewing, as you are very close to the Spirit of St. Louis Airport.

Artistic structures add a shady spot along the open trail.

County
St. Louis

Endpoints
Centaur Road west of N. Eatherton Road to Hardee's Iceplex on N. Outer 40 Road (Chesterfield)

Mileage
10.7

Type
Greenway/Non-Rail-Trail

Roughness Index
1

Surface
Asphalt

A retail shopping center comes into view as you near I-64. The trail heads under the interstate, but it's worth noting that there's a trail separated from traffic on the interstate bridge over the Missouri River that you could take to meet the Katy Trail State Park (see page 123) on the other side.

Once under the bridge, the trail takes you back on top of the levee and through the Chesterfield Valley Athletic Complex, where you'll find baseball diamonds, soccer fields, and plenty of parking. At this park is a rest area with benches and artistically designed shade structures, which are good to take advantage of as there's not much naturally occurring shade to be found on the levee. After another 3 miles of farm fields and retail establishments, you'll arrive at the end of this section of trail behind the Hardee's Iceplex.

Just on the other side of US 61/I-64, along Bonhomme Creek, is the shorter, 2.5-mile segment of the trail. Traveling east to west, this stretch of trail parallels Edison Avenue and allows easy access to a myriad of shopping, dining, and entertainment establishments that dominate this area. A mural greets trail users right after the Baxter Road crossing. While this trail is in a very busy area, the creek and surrounding riparian corridor allow for some interesting bird sightings along the way. The trail ends at a well-developed trailhead not far from a commercial area of the city.

CONTACT: **chesterfield.mo.us/monarch-levee-trail.html**

DIRECTIONS

The closest parking lot to the west end of the trail is located 4.2 miles east of the terminus. To reach the Chesterfield Valley Athletic Complex trailhead, from I-64, take Exit 14 toward Spirit of St. Louis Blvd. At the traffic circle, take the exit onto N. Outer 40 Road. Take an immediate turn north and then east into the athletic field parking area and trailhead.

To reach the Hardee's Iceplex trailhead from I-64, take Exit 17 for Boones Crossing and turn north. Turn east onto N. Outer 40 Road and go 0.9 mile to Hardee's Iceplex, on the north side of the road with the trailhead in the back.

To reach the Edison Ave. trailhead from I-64, take Exit 17 for Boones Crossing and turn south. Turn west onto Chesterfield Airport Road and travel 0.9 mile. Turn south onto Long Road. Go 0.3 mile and turn east onto Edison Avenue. The trailhead is immediately on the south side of the road.

The Riverfront Heritage Trail is located in the heart of Kansas City, Missouri. This downtown trail showcases the city's heritage, as well as its continuously redeveloping downtown areas. The trail also features connections that span west across the river into Kansas City, Kansas.

Begin your journey at the northern terminus, where the trail passes through the Richard L. Berkley Riverfront Park. The area was previously used as a landfill and an industrial site but is now reclaimed as a riverfront park and used for cultural events throughout the year. The trail's wide, smooth surface makes traveling through the park an easy experience. The perfect views of the Missouri River are not to be missed. You'll pass under the Heart of America Bridge and continue on your journey through the park, bearing right to stay on the trail. Interpretive signage tells the story and heritage of the Kansas City riverfront.

The Town of Kansas Bridge links the River Market to the Kansas City riverfront.

Counties
Jackson (MO), Wyandotte (KS)

Endpoints
N. Lydia Ave. just east of I-29 to Jefferson St. near Southwest Blvd. (Kansas City, MO) and Huron Park at the corner of Ann Ave. and N. 6th St. (Kansas City, KS)

Mileage
8.6

Type
Greenway/Non-Rail-Trail

Roughness Index
1

Surface
Asphalt, Concrete

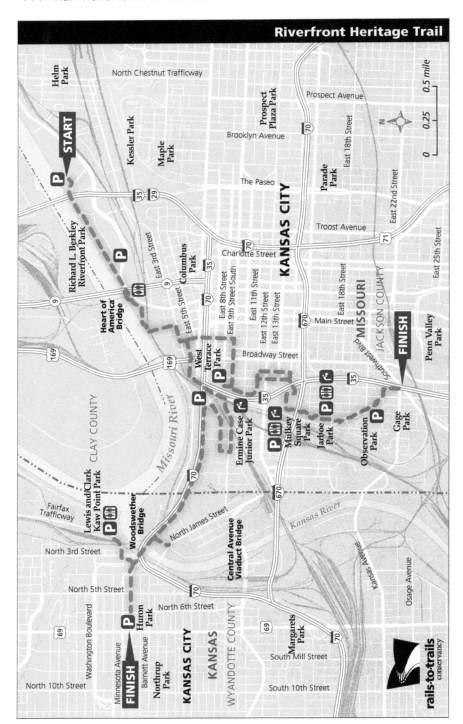

At the end of this riverside section of the trail, you'll come to the Town of Kansas Bridge. If the paved trail becomes broken and unpaved, you've missed the bridge and gone too far. To walk across the bridge, climb the stairs or take the elevator (hidden around the back side, near the stairs). Crossing the bridge, you'll arrive in the River Market district of downtown Kansas City, Missouri. Eateries are abundant in this area, and nearby museums and theaters provide cultural attractions.

Turn right onto West Third Street and follow the signs for the trail as it continues along the sidewalk. Turn left onto Wyandotte Street. Here, you may either turn right onto West Fourth Street to make the journey west into Kansas City, Kansas, or continue south into Kansas City, Missouri (see directions below). To head west, follow the trail down Beardsley Road and over Forrester Road. Turn right onto Hickory Street and right again onto Eighth Street as you ride through this industrial neighborhood of Kansas City. Be sure to ride to the Riverfront Heritage trailhead at the end of Eighth Street. The trailhead features a Santa Fe railcar and a commemoration of the area's history through four sculptures by a local artisan. The sculptures depict a slave family making their way toward Kansas, which was admitted to the United States as a free state without slavery in 1861. Interpretive signage commemorates the history and lives of African Americans who journeyed toward freedom.

From the trailhead, head north on Madison Avenue and follow the signage for the trail as it continues under I-70. As you enter into Kansas and cross the Woodswether Bridge, a new segment provides access to Lewis and Clark Kaw Point Park. Or continue on to reach the westernmost terminus of the trail at Huron Park.

Heading south in Kansas City, Missouri, from Wyandotte Street, continue south down Wyandotte Street by following signs for the trail. Take care as you turn right onto West Ninth Street, as this section is on-road and the last block goes up a steep hill; beginners may need to walk their bikes. Continue straight for seven blocks until you reach Ermine Case Junior Park, where water fountains are available. The trail picks up to the left, but be sure to check out the statue of Lewis and Clark, located to the right and down the street, where parking is available. Within the park, an overlook not far along the trail provides views of the train tracks and the west side of the city, still undergoing development.

Continue south on Kirk Drive as you exit the park; the roadway soon becomes W. 11th Street. You'll enter an on-road portion of the trail again as you turn right onto Pennsylvania for three blocks. Car traffic can be heavy, as cars enter the interstate from this stretch of road, so take care. At the intersection with West 14th Street, bear to the right and use the pedestrian bridge path to cross over I-35. After crossing the bridge, bear right as the trail loops around a baseball field and through Mulkey Square Park. Cross another pedestrian bridge over I-670 to arrive at Jarboe Park, which has a community swimming pool. Follow signs for the trail, as it alternates between an off-road path and on-road segments with sparse (if any) car traffic. The trail continues, paralleling West Pennway Street. At the intersection with Summit Street, cross the road to follow the trail, turning right to travel down the left-hand side of Jefferson Street for another block, where the trail ends.

CONTACT: **kcrivertrails.org**

DIRECTIONS

To reach the northern terminus at N. Lydia Ave. in Kansas City, MO, from I-29 N., take Exit 4 for Front Street/Grand Avenue. At the end of the exit, turn right onto Front St. and at the next intersection, turn left onto N. Lydia Ave. Turn right into the first parking lot.

To reach the western terminus at Huron Park in Kansas City, KS, from I-70 W, take Exit 423C. Keep left and follow the signs for Minnesota Ave. Turn left onto N. Fifth St. After two blocks, turn left onto Ann Ave. On-street parking is available in the area.

The Rock Island Spur extends Missouri's Katy Trail State Park (see page 123) by nearly 50 miles to the suburbs of Kansas City. At almost 240 miles, the famed Katy Trail spans nearly the entire state on a course through gorgeous Midwest countryside following the Missouri River.

The new rail-trail is named after the Rock Island Railroad, a company incorporated as the Rock Island & LaSalle Railroad Company in 1847. Mergers in the early 1900s saw the railway connecting Kansas City and St. Louis on opposite ends of Missouri. As railway traffic faded away, so too did the Rock Island Railroad. The last train on the tracks through Kansas City was seen in the early 1970s; by the 1980s, the rail corridor sat empty.

Though building a trail through the corridor is a massive undertaking and will require several years to complete, the project got off to an auspicious start with the opening of nearly 50 miles in 2016. This section,

The Katy Trail bridge in Windsor overlooks the Rock Island Spur.

Counties
Cass, Henry, Johnson

Endpoints
Katy Trail trailhead
(Windsor) to MO 58/
W. Commercial St. just
west of Walnut St.
(Pleasant Hill)

Mileage
46.2

Type
Rail-Trail

Roughness Index
1

Surface
Crushed Stone

Rock Island Spur of Katy Trail State Park

called the Rock Island Spur of Katy Trail State Park, is managed by Missouri State Parks. It begins at an intersection with the Katy Trail in the town of Windsor and takes users northwest to the city of Pleasant Hill.

The trail has a well-compacted, crushed-limestone surface best suited for hybrid bikes, though road bikes can also navigate the pathway. The difficulty for skinny tires would come after a rain when the trail's surface becomes soft. Equestrians can also ride the full length of the trail.

At the outset, you'll find a nod to the trail's railroad history with a caboose at the Windsor trailhead. As you continue onward, you'll discover that the trail's variety of terrains—wetlands, woodlands, and rolling farmland—makes it a pleasure to ride. About halfway through your journey, you'll come to the picturesque Rock Island Lake, where trains once stopped to fill their boilers.

At trail's end, you'll enter Pleasant Hill, which has a charming Downtown Historic District that's listed on the National Register of Historic Places, as well as colorful murals that depict the area's history and culture. Here, you'll find plentiful amenities for tourists, including antiques shops, arts and crafts boutiques, and cafés. History buffs will also want to stop in the Missouri Pacific Depot, a one-story brick building dating back to 1903; inside you'll find information on local trails and the trains that once ran through the region.

A future segment will continue the trail's northwestern trajectory through Jackson County to the outskirts of Kansas City, where it will end at the Truman Sports Complex, home to the NFL's Chiefs and MLB's Royals. On its opposite end, another future segment will head eastward from Windsor, stretching a whopping 144 miles to the town of Beaufort before angling northeast to meet up again with the Katy Trail near the town of Washington.

CONTACT: **mostateparks.com/park/rock-island-spur**

DIRECTIONS

To reach the eastern trailhead in Windsor from Kansas City, take I-70 eastward. Take Exit 58 for MO 23 and follow it south for 39 miles to a T-intersection with MO 2. Turn left onto MO 2, and travel 2.7 miles to the outskirts of Windsor; as the highway enters town, it becomes W. Benton St. Turn left onto Mill St., then take the next left onto W. Florence St. and you'll see the parking area immediately to your right.

Near the trail's western terminus, you'll find parking at Pleasant Hill's restored train depot (100 Wyoming St.). To reach the depot from I-49, take Exit 174 for MO 58. Turn right (east) onto MO 58 and travel the highway for 14 miles to Pleasant Hill. In town, the highway becomes W. Commercial St. Take a left onto Broadway St. and you'll immediately see the building and parking area. From there, walk or ride 0.3 mile southwest on-road or on sidewalks to reach the trail near the intersection of W. Commercial Street and Walnut Street.

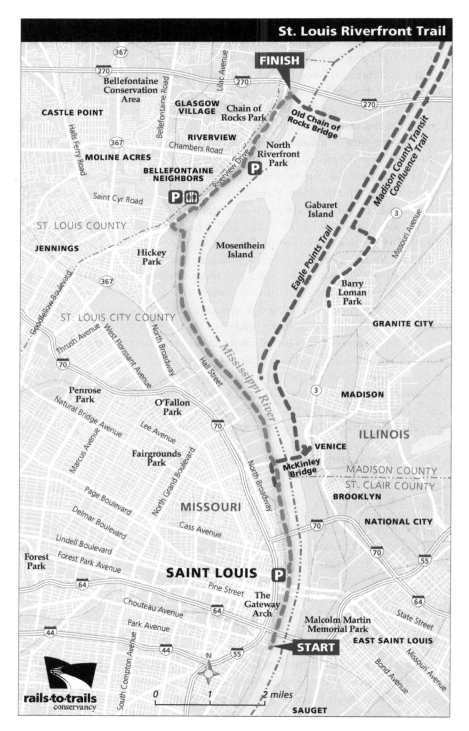

St. Louis Riverfront Trail

When you think of St. Louis, some iconic images likely come to mind: the Mississippi River, the Gateway Arch, and Lewis and Clark. The St. Louis Riverfront Trail lets you experience all of this and more! Starting just south of the Gateway Arch in downtown, this paved trail is a must-visit.

You begin with what is known locally as the "graffiti wall" along the left side of the trail; its expressive colors and artwork make you want to slow down. On the east side of the trail is the majestic Mississippi River. The trail goes along the riverfront and right next to the Gateway Arch as you pass by downtown. Multiple excursion opportunities dot the trail, from classic sternwheeler riverboat rides to helicopter tours, through this section. If history is your interest, the Lewis and Clark statue on the river adjacent to the trail is worth a stop.

Moving north from downtown, the first well-branded trailhead emerges under the shadows of the former Union

Adjacent to the trailhead is the former Union Electric Light and Power Company building circa 1903.

County
St. Louis

Endpoints
S. Leonor K. Sullivan Blvd. and Chouteau Ave. to Riverview Dr. at the Old Chain of Rocks Bridge (St. Louis)

Mileage
12.2

Type
Greenway/Non-Rail-Trail

Roughness Index
1

Surface
Asphalt

Power generating station, which is a historical and beautiful building. The transition of the trail from the bustling downtown area to a more industrial landscape is done tastefully and is an example of well-designed trail development in constricted areas. The large concrete flood walls that are a constant along the river also provide the backdrop for numerous art installations.

The trail takes a meandering path—at times on the inside of the levee, at other times outside the walls—and sometimes you get right on top for a wonderful view of both the working riverfront and the industry that still relies on the storied waterway. Multiple rest stops along the way offer bike racks, interpretive signage, and drinking water.

This stretch offers an interesting opportunity to watch the relationship between the river and industry. Large tugboats push barges with all sorts of cargo as trains run up and down the tracks to a multitude of different commodity industries ready to load or offload the barges. Leaving the heavier industry behind, a few miles of quieter trail let you just enjoy the river and a couple of nice parks before you emerge to one last icon at the end of the trail. The Old Chain of Rocks Bridge marks the northern end of the Riverfront Trail. Part of the historical Route 66, the mile-long bike and pedestrian crossing of the Mississippi River reaches Illinois on the other side.

CONTACT: **greatriversgreenway.org/greenway /mississippi-greenway-chouteau-old-chain-of-rocks-bridge**

DIRECTIONS

To reach downtown St. Louis parking from I-55, take Exit 40 for I-44 toward I-70/Kansas St./ Walnut St. Follow signs for I-70 W/Kansas City and merge onto I-44. Take Exit 292 toward Washington Ave./Eads Bridge. Continue onto Memorial Drive; then turn west onto Washington Ave. Turn left onto Fourth St., then right onto Convention Plaza/Dr. Martin Luther King Jr. Bridge. Take an immediate right turn onto Laclede's Landing Blvd., and then take a right to head south onto Commercial St. A parking garage is on the left. One block away, toward the river, you can walk or bike to the trail, which parallels S. Leonor K. Sullivan Blvd.

To reach the northern trailhead from I-270, take Exit 34 for Riverview Drive and go south 1.7 miles. Turn left onto Spring Garden Drive. The trailhead and parking are located in North Riverfront Park. The Old Chain of Rocks Bridge lies 1.2 miles north of the park and is reachable via the Riverfront Trail.

The Urban Trail system in St. Joseph is a suburban jewel, with lush, green scenery along most of its route. The system branches off in several directions, offering a number of customizable routes for a shorter or longer trail experience. Sections of the trail feature steep hills; some may wish to walk their bikes up these sections, but the climbs are never long and the downhill experience on the opposite side is worth the trek.

Hyde Park marks the start of your journey on the Urban Trail system. There are two parking lots at either end of the park; the trail begins at the westernmost end, featuring a wrought iron gate with the name of the park. Note: There are trail paths in the park, but instead of taking those, you will need to cross Mason Road to begin your journey.

This section of the trail parallels Southwest Parkway, with well-marked crosswalks as the trail cuts across the

The Urban Trail provides a safe route through Saint Joseph and features this pedestrian bridge over a busy highway.

County
Buchanan

Endpoints
E. Hyde Park Ave. and Southwest Pkwy. to Ferndale Ave. and Northwest Pkwy. and S. Riverside Road just north of Beechwood Blvd. (St. Joseph)

Mileage
15.8

Type
Greenway/Non-Rail-Trail

Roughness Index
1

Surface
Asphalt, Concrete

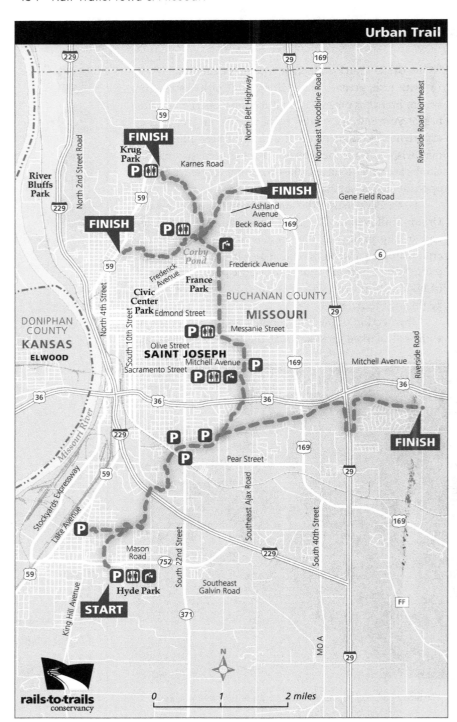

Urban Trail

The Urban Trail is a suburban jewel, with lush, green scenery along most of its route.

parkway. Greenery is abundant in this section, though shade cover is sparse. The trail continues to wind its way through the parkway, meandering up and down hills. Some are steep and may require walking a bike, but the downhill coast on the well-maintained concrete trail is a smooth ride.

The trail crosses under I-229 and continues through a green landscape. After the next separated-path bridge crossing, the route passes through a residential area, with a recreation center on the left. You'll soon reach a roundabout with red brick. For a longer trail experience, bear left and continue north (directions below).

Heading east: For a shorter trail experience, bear right and continue on. On this section, suburban homes peek through the trees and, as the trail curves to the right, it parallels I-29. An off-street bridge connection will take you over I-29. At the next street intersection, turn left to head down South Leonard Road. At the end of the road, the trail enters a tree-lined area; from here on, the lush green landscape never leaves the trail. The route alternates between open and shaded sections and features a scenic trestle bridge. The trail ends at the intersection with busy South Riverside Road.

Heading north: After bearing left at the roundabout, you'll continue your journey north through a green park area. The trail passes under US 36 and continues to parallel Southwest Parkway. After passing through a local park, there is a short on-street connection through a low-speed residential neighborhood for less than half a mile. At the end of the road, turn left onto Parkway A and follow the bike route signs to pick up the trail. Bear to the right and continue down North Noyes Boulevard for 1.3 miles. At the busy multiway intersection with Ashland Avenue, cross the street first and then turn right onto Ashland Avenue. Keep your eyes peeled for the entrance to the trail, marked by two low brick walls. If you reach the next cross streets—Crescent Drive or Hundley Drive—you've gone too far.

In this section, the trail travels through a town park, with plenty of trees and shaded areas. You'll come to a four-way intersection with the option to continue north or travel the east-west corridor of the trail system (directions below).

Heading north: Continue straight on, passing through the park into a residential area. Bear right at Lover's Lane and take care while crossing the unmarked intersection to pick up the trail for another three-quarters of a mile. The trail ends where it intersects with Ferndale Avenue.

East-west corridor: Turning right at the intersection, the corridor travels along a linear park with a few hills and lots of greenery and shade. The segment ends where it meets Ashland Avenue, about a mile up the trail. Turning left at the intersection, the corridor soon enters a short off-road portion, crossing North 22nd Street with Corby Pond on the left, before picking up the trail again. Paralleling Corby Parkway, the trail passes through a suburban area for a little over a mile, eventually reaching a park on Mapleleaf Boulevard where the trail ends.

CONTACT: stjoemo.info/index.aspx?NID=253

DIRECTIONS

To reach the Hyde Park trailhead, from I-229, take Exit 3. Head south on S. 22nd St. and turn right onto Mason Road for a little over a mile. Hyde Park is on the left with a large iron gate marking the entrance. There is some parking at this entrance and some parking at the other end of the park, as well.

To reach the northernmost terminus close to the intersection of Ferndale Ave. and Northwest Pkwy., head north on St. Joseph Ave./US 59. Turn right at the exit for Northwest Pkwy., just before Karnes Road. Turn left onto Ferndale Ave. and the trail is on the right. A few parking spots and on-street parking are available.

Index

Presented by

rails·to·trails
conservancy

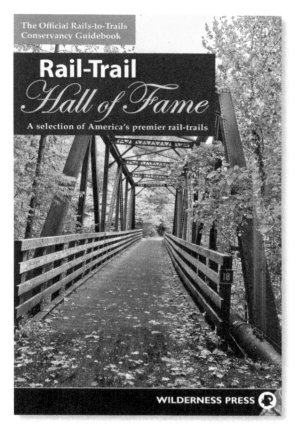

Rail-Trail Hall of Fame

ISBN: 978-0-89997-825-3   152 pages, full-color
$16.95, 1st Edition   maps and photos

Explore premier rail-trails across America with this official guide. In 2007 Rails-to-Trails Conservancy began recognizing exemplary rail-trails through its Rail-Trail Hall of Fame.

These Hall of Fame rail-trails are found in 28 states and in nearly every environment—from downtown urban corridors to pathways stretching across wide-open prairie, along coastlines, or through mountain ranges.

Rail-Trails: Illinois, Indiana & Ohio

ISBN: 978-0-89997-848-2
$18.95, 1st Edition

272 pages, full-color
maps and photos

Explore 72 of the best rail-trails and multiuse pathways across three states. Tour Ohio's Amish country, take a ride along Chicago's lakefront, and enjoy the picturesque countryside on Indiana's longest rail-trail. These adventures and more await you on the many multiuse trails of the Midwest!

Presented by

rails·to·trails
conservancy

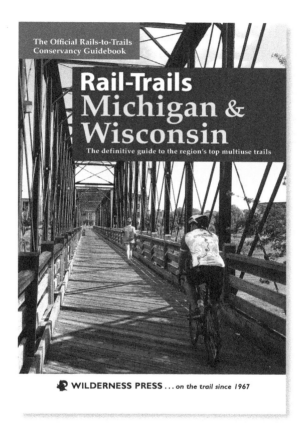

Rail-Trails: Michigan & Wisconsin

ISBN: 978-0-89997-873-4
$18.95, 1st Edition

264 pages, full-color
maps and photos

Explore 63 of the best rail-trails and multiuse pathways across two states. Discover Wisconsin's iconic Elroy-Sparta State Trail—widely acknowledged to be the oldest rail-trail in America—or Lake Michigan Pathway, which features beaches and marinas that will keep you in close touch with its namesake. You'll love the variety in this collection of Midwestern multiuse trails—from beautiful waterways and scenic areas to the hustle and bustle of the states' urban centers.

Photo Credits

Page iii: Eli Griffen; *page 7:* Martha Wicker; *page 9:* Joe LaCroix; *page 11:* Eli Griffen; *page 15:* Laura Stark; *page 19:* Eli Griffen; *page 21:* Laura Stark; *page 25:* Eli Griffen; *page 27:* Joe LaCroix; *page 30:* Joe LaCroix; *page 31:* Suzanne Matyas; *page 35:* Eli Griffen; *page 39:* Liz Sewell; *page 40:* Liz Sewell; *page 43:* Milo Bateman; *page 45:* Milo Bateman; *page 47:* Ryan Cree; *page 48:* Ryan Cree; *page 51:* Brandi Horton; *page 53:* Suzanne Matyas; *page 57:* Joe LaCroix; *page 59:* Milo Bateman; *page 61:* Milo Bateman; *page 63:* Milo Bateman; *page 67:* Laura Stark; *page 68:* Laura Stark; *page 71:* Laura Stark; *page 73:* Laura Stark; *page 77:* Eli Griffen; *page 79:* Joe LaCroix; *page 83:* Elton Clark; *page 85:* Ryan Cree; *page 89:* Suzanne Matyas; *page 91:* Laura Stark; *page 95:* Joe LaCroix; *page 99:* Joe LaCroix; *page 103:* Milo Bateman; *page 105:* Eli Griffen; *page 107:* Wilson Hurst; *page 109:* Leeann Sinpatanasakul; *page 111:* Brian Housh; *page 115:* courtesy of the Joplin Trails Coalition; *page 117:* Katie Guerin; *page 121:* Brian Housh; *page 123:* Danielle Taylor; *page 126:* courtesy of Missouri State Parks; *page 127:* Katie Guerin; *page 131:* Katie Guerin; *page 133:* Eric Oberg; *page 137:* courtesy of Columbia Parks and Recreation; *page 141:* Eric Oberg; *page 143:* Leeann Sinpatanasakul; *page 147:* courtesy of Missouri Rock Island Trail, Inc.; *page 151:* Eric Oberg; *page 153:* Leeann Sinpatanasakul; *page 155:* Leeann Sinpatanasakul.

Support Rails-to-Trails Conservancy

The nation's leader in helping communities transform unused rail lines and connecting corridors into multiuse trails, Rails-to-Trails Conservancy (RTC) depends on the support of its members and donors to create access to healthy outdoor experiences.

Your donation will help support programs and services that have helped put more than 22,000 rail-trail miles on the ground. Every day, RTC provides vital assistance to communities to develop and maintain trails throughout the country. In addition, RTC advocates for trail-friendly policies, promotes the benefits of rail-trails, and defends rail-trail laws in the courts.

Join online at railstotrails.org, or mail your donation to Rails-to-Trails Conservancy, 2121 Ward Court NW, Fifth Floor, Washington, DC 20037.

Rails-to-Trails Conservancy is a 501(c)(3) nonprofit organization, and contributions are tax deductible.

Find your next trail adventure on TrailLink

Visit TrailLink.com today.

TrailLink
by Rails-to-Trails Conservancy

CPSIA information can be obtained
at www.ICGtesting.com
Printed in the USA
BVHW010945210520
580080BV00002B/5